INSIGHT COMPACT GUIDES

Cape Cod

W9-AVQ-370

Compact Guide: Cape Cod is the ideal quick reference guide to this much loved part of New England. It tells you all you need to know about Cape Cod's attractions, from historic towns to the lovely National Seashore, from churches, lighthouses and windmills to the best freshwater ponds and clam shacks.

This is just one title in *Apa Publications'* new series of pocket-sized, easy-to-use guidebooks intended for the independent-minded traveler. *Compact Guides* pride themselves on being up-to-date and authoritative. They are in essence mini travel encyclopedias, designed to be comprehensive yet portable, as well as readable and reliable.

Star Attractions

An instant reference
to some of Cape
Cod's most popular
tourist attractions
to help you on
your way.

*Sandwich Glass
Museum p16*

*Nobska Light, Woods
Hole p22*

*West Parish Meeting-
house, Barnstable p27*

*JFKennedy Museum,
Hyannis p29*

*First Parish Church,
Brewster p36*

Chatham Fish Pier p39

*Rock Harbor, Orleans
p42*

*Nauset Light Beach,
Eastham p42*

*Highland
Light, Truro
p48*

*Provincetown Art
Association p52*

Plimoth Plantation p55

CapeCod

Introduction

Places

Culture

Leisure

Practical Information

Cape Cod – A Great Escape

Cape Cod has a special place in the hearts and minds of Americans. Not only does it embody the perfect summer vacation of long sandy beaches, clear ocean water and hot sunny days, but it also carries many diverse associations: the Pilgrims who spent their first month in the New World anchored in Provincetown Harbor; the 19th-century whaling ships which sailed around the world from Cape Cod ports; the Kennedy clan ensconced in their Hyannis compound; the Cape Cod house, the most popular style of home in the United States; the native cranberry, indispensable on any Thanksgiving table; and Edward Hopper's paintings of stark, sundrenched beaches.

Recurrent themes: the lighthouse and the church

People from all walks of life are drawn here, from the wealthy with their summer homes to struggling artists spending a cold but inspired winter. There are some who still earn a living from the sea and others who live year round off their earnings from the tourist season. Old New England families live side by side with Portuguese fishermen, famous writers, gay couples and newly-arrived 'year-rounders' escaping the pressures of modern city life.

5

A visitor to Cape Cod will find both stunning natural beauty and a rich cultural history. There are 30 miles (50km) of pristine Atlantic beach within the National Seashore plus a rich diversity of landscape and wildlife throughout the peninsula. Salt marshes, pine groves, open moors, small rivers, ponds and harbors are all accessible by trails, bike paths and small roads. Cape Cod's cultural history is also easily accessible. Vestiges of 350 years of European habitation and of a Native American Indian population for thousands of years before that are preserved in the many designated historic districts on the Cape.

When life's a beach

Over the past century, the Cape has inspired visual artists and writers. Eugene O'Neill, Jackson Pollock, Mark Rothko and Norman Mailer are just a few. Called the birthplace of modern American theater, the Cape maintains a thriving tradition for live performance.

Location

Thrust 70 miles (112km) out to sea, Cape Cod juts further into the Atlantic than any other part of the United States. Likened to the shape of a bent arm, the peninsula sits 50 miles (80km) southeast of Boston and 200 miles (320km) east of New York City. Four bodies of water surround the Cape: Buzzard's Bay to the West, Nantucket Sound to the South, the Atlantic Ocean to the East, and Cape Cod Bay enclosed within the curl of the peninsula. Since the digging of the Cape Cod Canal in 1914, the peninsula has effectively been an island.

The 15 towns of Cape Cod are divided into three sections, Upper, Mid and Lower or Outer, referring to the latitudes used in the days of sailing. Upper is near the canal, and includes Sandwich, Bourne, Falmouth and Mashpee. Mid Cape encompasses Barnstable, Yarmouth and Dennis. The Lower Cape stretches from the 'elbow' at Brewster to the tip at Provincetown, although the Outer Cape is often differentiated from the Lower, and includes Eastham, Wellfleet, Truro and Provincetown.

Geography and geology

Cape Cod is the world's largest glacial peninsula, formed during the final great ice age that covered New England from about 25,000 years ago until 17,000 years ago. Glacial deposits make up the land as far as Pilgrim Heights in Truro, past which the land has been created by shifting sand, effectively making Provincetown one enormous sand bar. The many kettle ponds on the Cape were formed by huge chunks of ice left by a retreating glacier.

Cape Cod was originally heavily wooded. The early settlers cleared land for farming and used many of the large trees for building and as fuel for local industries. The area has always been a place of extremes. Tides can rise as high as 9ft (3 meters) and tidal flats can stretch a mile out to sea. The summer tends to be peaceful and calm, but come October raging gales can dramatically change the landscape, sometimes in a matter of hours.

Steady erosion eats away an average of 2–3 acres (0.8–1.2 hectares) of coastline a year. It is along the outer beach of the National Seashore, where the great bluffs face the open ocean, that this erosion is most visible. For 15 miles (24km), sand bluffs line the beach, rising from 30ft (9 meters) to as high as 170ft (52 meters) above the sea. Sand continuously shifts down the slope of the dunes, and waves sometimes pull down whole sections at once.

Outer beach cliffs
Stormy weather

The waters around the Cape have always been dangerous for shipping. Before the canal was built, boats had to circumnavigate the peninsula, risking the treacherous shoals surrounding Cape Cod. Over 3,000 ships have been wrecked off these shores since the 1600s. Cape Cod Canal has greatly reduced the danger and some 30,000 vessels a year use this passageway

Climate and when to go

The summer season runs roughly from the Fourth of July to Memorial Day. Most of the small Cape museums and attractions are only open during this time, with some limited hours in June and September. The 'season' has been extending, however, with some facilities opening in spring and staying open weekends well into October or until Thanksgiving.

Off season on the Cape is a peaceful time when year-round residents recover from the hectic summer. The fall is loved for its sparkling light and vibrant foliage. Though it cannot compete with the brilliant mountainsides of other parts of New England, it has its own magic, especially when the cranberries are harvested. Winter can be fierce with the onset of some tremendous storms: it can also be quiet with less snow than on the mainland. Winter is long, however, with a brief spring arriving in May or even as late as June. Summer weather tends to be hot and sunny.

Summer fun
Wild at heart

Population

There were five tribes of Native Americans inhabiting the Cape when the Pilgrims arrived. Each had its own sachem (chief), who was in turn ruled by a great sachem who headed the Wampanoag Federation and lived near what is now Providence, Rhode Island. The Indian population, about 40,000 in the Federation in 1600, was drastically reduced first by European diseases brought by explorers and then by the rapid takeover of their land by settlers. Today there are barely 600 Wampanoags living in the town of Mashpee, the first Indian reservation in America.

Although small fleets from Portugal, Holland and the Basque country had been fishing off these coasts as early as the 16th century, the first settlers were English. Many old New England families trace their roots to these early inhabitants. The Portuguese came on the whaling ships of the 19th century and still make up a large number of the population. The most significant change to the Cape's population, though, has been the influx of summer visitors, brought here first by the new railroad in the late 19th century and then by car. With the increasing accessibility of Cape Cod to Boston and Providence, the year-round population has risen over the past 30 years from 70,000 to 190,000. During the summer months this figure triples.

The sachem Massasoit

Whaling in the 19th century
Captain's house

The cod fish

Economy

The first settlers concentrated their efforts on farming, since this is what they had known back home. However, with the thin layer of top soil eroding quickly, early Cape Codders soon turned to the sea for their livelihood. On-shore whaling, taught to them by the native Indians, proved lucrative until, by the 1750s, whales had been chased too far out to sea. Whaling progressed to deep-sea vessels which roamed the oceans on voyages lasting up to four years. The whaling heyday lasted from 1825 to 1860, and throughout the Cape one can still see mansions built by the captains who made their fortunes from whales.

Fishing was always the true bread and butter of the Cape Codder. Before the age of refrigeration, salt fish was the dietary mainstay of most of America's poor and many Cape towns grew rich from the industry. Vessels, called bankers, would leave for several months at a time, heading to two areas naturally rich in fish, Grand Banks, off the coast of Newfoundland, and George's Bank, closer to Cape Cod though more dangerous. A triangular trade developed as early as 1730, with boats taking fish, salted on board, to the Caribbean and returning with rum and molasses in exchange. The salt fish industry employed most of the local population in related trades, from shipbuilders, sailmakers, coopers and blacksmiths to the boys and old men who put the catch out to dry on fish flakes.

The Industrial Revolution spelled the end of salt fish on Cape Cod since competition demanded greater capital than the small Cape towns possessed. They turned to trap and weir fishing, and to local shellfish harvesting. Today there are several small but tenacious fleets which sail from local harbors, but smaller quotas, declining stocks, expensive equipment and competition from the 'factory ships' of foreign countries make it a hard way to earn a living.

By the end of the 19th century, the population had been drastically reduced by the lack of local prospects and the lure of employment in nearby cities. It was the advent of the railroad and the beginning of tourism which rescued Cape Cod from economic depression.

The past 30 years has seen enormous development throughout the Cape. Since the beginning of the 1990s, concern about this unchecked growth has produced agencies devoted to preserving the Cape's fragile environment and wildlife. With the increase in real estate prices, Cape communities have also been under threat, since local people can't always afford the prices wealthy summer visitors are willing to pay. A number of schemes to aid residents are now under way to help safeguard the diversity of population that makes Cape Cod unique.

One local commodity which still flourishes is the cranberry, first grown commercially in Harwich in the 1840s. Massachusetts is now the largest cranberry producer in the world. The local harvest accounts for 10 percent of the state's produce.

Flora and fauna

Beach rose 9

The most significant action to safeguard Cape Cod's fragile natural environment was the formation of the Cape Cod National Seashore in 1961. From Chatham to Provincetown, 44,000 acres (17,800 hectares) were set aside as protected land. This area is unusual for a Federal Park in that it encompasses beautiful natural environments alongside historic homes, lighthouses and coastguard stations.

The Cape is home to a wide variety of marine, plant and animal life. Cape Cod Bay, affected by the cold water from the Gulf of Maine and the Labrador Current is on average 10°F (4.4°C) colder than Nantucket Sound, which is warmed by the Gulf Stream. This differentiation creates two distinct marine environments, and has helped to produce one of the richest marine habitats on the East Coast.

For visitors, the favorite inhabitants of the nearby waters are probably the whales who visit every spring and fall and feed on the nearby Stellwagon Bank. Among the marine mammals most commonly seen are humpback, fin, right and minke whales, as well as white-sided dolphins. Harbor seals spend the winter months on some of the Atlantic beaches of the Outer Cape and rare gray seals have been sighted on Monomoy Island.

Marine visitors

Cape Cod also offers some of the best bird-watching on the East Coast. More than 350 species have been seen here, ranging from sea birds to hawks and falcons. Foxes, deer, racoons, opossum and coyotes are only some of the animals that live here. The variety of plant life reflects the range of natural habitats, and even in the seemingly barren sand dunes lovely wildflowers can be found in spring.

Historical Highlights

23,000–15,000BC Cape Cod is formed by glacial deposits left by the last great ice age to cover New England.

7,000BC The first native inhabitants arrive, leading a primarily nomadic life.

1500s Fishing fleets from Europe take advantage of the fish surrounding Cape Cod, returning to Europe with boatloads of salted fish.

The Wampanoag Federation of Indian Tribes inhabiting what is now eastern Massachusetts, Naraguansett Bay and Cape Cod, number 40,000–60,000.

1602 Bartholomew Gosnold explores Cape Cod and names it after the large schools of codfish he finds here.

1606 Samuel de Champlain lands in Stage Harbor, Chatham, and is fought off by Indians from the Eastham area.

1614 Captain Thomas Hunt kidnaps 24 Wampanoag Indians and sells them into slavery in Spain. One of these is Squanto who eventually returns to New England and becomes an indispensable friend and interpreter to the Plymouth settlement.

1617–18 Plague brought by white men kills large numbers of Native Americans.

November 9, 1620 The Pilgrims arrive in Provincetown Harbor aboard the *Mayflower* after two months at sea. It is here that they draw up the *Mayflower Compact*, the first document of self-governance in the New World. Four days later the Pilgrims discover a cache of corn in Truro which helps them survive their first winter in Plymouth. On December 7, Myles Standish's exploring party is awoken on a beach in Eastham by raining arrows from local Indians. On December 16, the *Mayflower* passengers head to nearby Plymouth.

December 17, 1626 The *Sparrowhawk*, carrying immigrants to Plymouth, is the first recorded ship to wreck off the shore of Cape Cod. Over 3,000 boats suffer the same fate during the next 370 years.

1627 Aptuxet Trading Post is established, the first English-speaking trading post in North America.

1637 The town of Sandwich is incorporated, the first town on Cape Cod.

1660 Plantation of Mashpee, the country's first Indian Reservation, is set up by Richard Bourne.

1675 King Philip's War, a bloody Indian uprising, rages across New England. However, Cape Cod is spared, mainly due to Richard Bourne's amicable relations with the Indians of Mashpee Plantation

1730 By now a triangular trade has developed whereby Cape Cod fishermen transport salted fish to the Caribbean and return to New England with rum and molasses.

1761 In a fiery four-hour speech in Boston, James Otis, Jr, from Barnstable, is the first to vocalize resistance to British authorities.

1774 1,500 citizens march on the Barnstable Courthouse and prevent the opening of His Majesty's Court.

1776–83 Many Cape Codders are involved in fighting against the British, primarily at sea. Cape Cod is blockaded by British ships throughout the war, creating much hardship.

1787 John Kendrick of Harwich captains the *Columbia*, the first American ship to circumnavigate the globe.

1797 Highland Light, Cape Cod's first lighthouse, is erected in Truro.

1812–15 The War of 1812 is very unpopular on Cape Cod and is supported by only two towns, Falmouth and Orleans. Once again the peninsula is blockaded by the British.

December 19, 1814 The Battle of Rock Harbor takes place. The British *HMS Newcastle* is repulsed by the Orleans militia. This is one of the few battles of the War of 1812 to take place on Cape soil.

1821 George's Bank, with its rich stores of fish, opens up to local fishing fleets, providing much closer, although more dangerous, fishing grounds than Newfoundland's Grand Banks.

1825 The Boston and Sandwich Glass Company is founded by Demming Jarvis.

1825–60 The whaling industry is at its peak, creating large fortunes for those involved. Courage and knowledge are needed to survive voyages which can last up to four years.

1840s Commercial cultivation of cranberries begins in Harwich.

October 1841 A terrible gale destroys Cape Cod's fishing fleets. Truro is the worst hit, with seven out of the town's eight vessels destroyed and 57 men and boys drowned.

1848 The Cape Cod Branch Railroad arrives at Sandwich (extending to Provincetown by 1873), bringing with it 'Summer People,' the area's first tourists.

1864 Posthumous publication of Henry David Thoreau's *Cape Cod*, recounting his exploration of the Lower Cape between 1849–55.

1865 After the Civil War, whaling and salt fishing move to the larger ports off-Cape and many of the population head west or to industrial centers. This leads to a drastic decline in the local economy, saved only by the growing number of summer tourists towards the end of the century.

1871 US Commission of Fish and Fisheries sets up a seasonal collecting station in Woods Hole and establishes the country's first aquarium there.

1879 The first Transatlantic cable is laid from Brest, France, to St Pierre, Newfoundland and on to Nauset Beach. In 1898 a direct cable is laid from Brest to Town Cove in Orleans.

1899 Charles Hawthorne opens his Cape Cod School of Art in Provincetown, the area's first art school. By 1916, there are six art schools in town.

January 19, 1903 The first US transatlantic wireless telegraph communication is transmitted from Marconi's station in Wellfleet from President Theodore Roosevelt to King Edward VII.

1907 President Theodore Roosevelt attends the laying of the corner stone of the Pilgrim Monument in Provincetown.

July 29, 1914 The Cape Cod Canal is completed with opening ceremonies attended by Franklin D. Roosevelt, Secretary of the Navy at the time.

1915–16 The Provincetown Players, a co-operative theater group, performs in Provincetown for two summers, premiering Eugene O'Neill's *Bound East For Cardiff*.

1918 A German U-Boat fires on small boats off the shore of Orleans, the only place in the continental USA to come under enemy fire in either World War. Servicemen of the nearby Chatham Airforce base are at the time playing baseball in Provincetown so retaliation is ineffectual.

1920s Paved roads are constructed down-Cape, bringing the first visitors by automobile.

1926 Joe and Rose Kennedy spend the summer in a small cottage in Hyannis, the beginning of the Kennedy Compound. In 1956 Senator John F. Kennedy buys the house adjacent to his parents', which becomes the Summer White House.

1926–7 Henry Beston spends a year in a house in the dunes of Nauset Beach, recounting his observations in *The Outermost House*.

1930 The Cape Cinema opens in Dennis with the world premier of *The Wizard of Oz*.

August 7, 1961 The Cape Cod National Seashore is created by an act of Congress.

1968 The Fine Arts Work Center is founded to provide emerging artists and writers with a chance to live and work in Provincetown.

1976 The Center for Coastal Studies is set up in Provincetown.

January 1987 A fierce northeaster creates a breach in the barrier beach protecting Chatham Harbor, destroying waterfront properties.

1996 Highland Light is moved 200ft (60 meters) from the cliff edge to save it from erosion. Nauset Light is earmarked for a similar move.

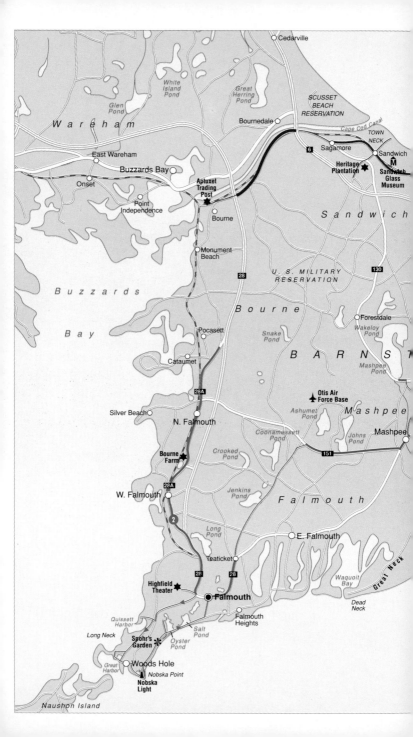

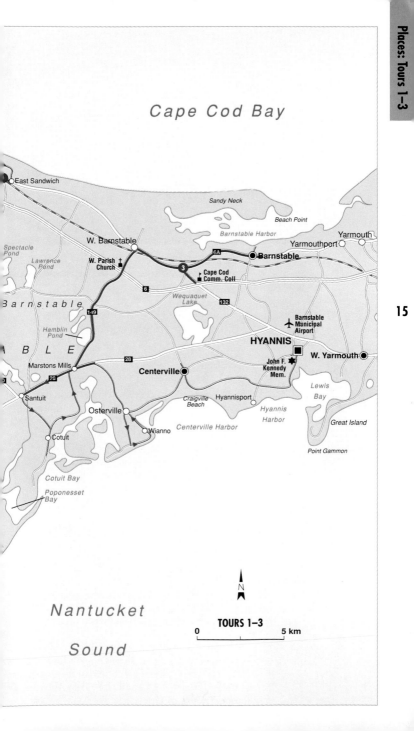

Cape Cod Bay

East Sandwich

Sandy Neck

Beach Point

Barnstable Harbor

Yarmouth

W. Barnstable

Yarmouthport

Spectacle
Pond

Lawrence
Pond

6A

Barnstable

W. Parish
Church

3

Cape Cod
Comm. Coll

6

B a r n s t a b l e

Wequaquet
Lake

132

Barnstable
Municipal
Airport

1-49

Hamblin
Pond

A B L E

HYANNIS

W. Yarmouth

28

Marstons Mills

Centerville

John F.
Kennedy
Mem.

28

Lewis
Bay

Santuit

Osterville

Craigville
Beach

Hyannisport

Hyannis
Harbor

Great Island

Cotuit

Wianno

Centerville Harbor

Point Gammon

Cotuit Bay

Poponesset
Bay

N

Nantucket

TOURS 1–3

0   5 km

Sound

Sandwich town center
Previous pages: cottages along
Cape Cod Bay

Tour 1

Cape Cod's Oldest Town

Sandwich town center – Heritage Plantation – Cape Cod Canal – Aptuxet Trading Post

Sandwich is the first town on Cape Cod both geographically and historically. It was here in 1637 that the first group of English colonists, the 'tenn men of Saugust' chose to settle, given permission by the Plymouth Colony to 'view a place to sitt down and have sufficient lands for three score families.' When incorporated in 1639, the town chose the name of Sandwich after the English town from which many of the settlers had recently come.

The spot was rich in local resources, with good fishing, forests full of lumber, fresh water and plentiful salt marshes for fodder. Some of these same resources attracted Demming Jarvis to set up glass manufacturing here in 1825. The Boston and Sandwich Glass Company, as it was called, did not use the local sand for production, since it was too rich in iron, but did take advantage of the abundant forests to fuel the glass furnaces, and grass from the salt marshes as packing material for the fragile product.

Sandwich today is a peaceful backwater. Devoid of commercialization, the old town center comprises mill pond and grist mill surrounded by old clapboard and shingled houses, with several interesting museums.

Find your way to the center of town, at the intersection of Main and Water streets. Here is Shawme Pond and the Dexter Grist Mill, with the old Town Hall, the First Church of Christ and the ★★★ **Sandwich Glass Museum ❶** (open 1 April to 31 October, daily 9.30am–4.30pm, No-

Proud of its past
Sandwich glass

vember to December and February to March, Wednesday to Sunday 9:30am–4pm), the best place to start your exploration. The museum offers a detailed account of the history of the Boston and Sandwich Glass Company (1825–88) and the Cape Cod Glass Works (1859–69).

The **Town Hall** ❷ (c1834) and the **Dexter Grist Mill** ❸ are on **Shawme Pond**. Built in the mid-1600s, the mill has served many functions, from turning a turbine during the town's glass-making heyday to serving as a tea room in the 1920s. Restored in 1961, it now has a resident miller in the summer who demonstrates how corn was ground. Across Water Street from the mill is the **First Church of Christ** ❹. Founded in 1638, it is the oldest congregation on Cape Cod, and the present church was built in 1847. Search out its brass bell inside, cast in 1675 and one of the oldest in the country.

A little further down Main Street, on the corner of River Street, stands ★ **Yesteryears Doll Museum** ❺ (open mid-May to mid-October, Monday to Saturday 10am–4pm), housed in the former First Parish Meetinghouse. Parts of the building date back as early as 1638, and the stained-glass windows are made of Sandwich glass donated by Demming Jarvis. Inside is a wonderful collection of old dolls from around the world, spanning three centuries.

Head back to the First Church of Christ and turn left onto Water Street, following the bank of Shawme Pond. The ★★ **Thornton W. Burgess Museum** ❻ (open year round Monday to Saturday 10am–4pm, Sunday 1–4pm), at 4 Water Street, is dedicated to the author of the beloved Peter Cottontail books. Born in Sandwich in 1874, and author of more than 15,000 stories and 170 books, Burgess was also a dedicated naturalist. The museum houses his

Shawme Pond

17

Peter Cottontail

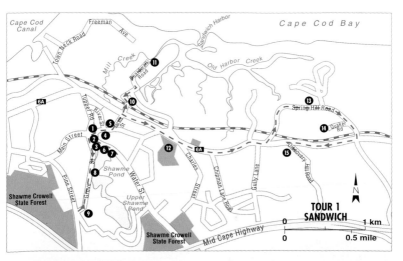

TOUR 1
SANDWICH

The Hoxie House

The boardwalk
Heritage Plantation carousel

extensive book collection as well as originals of Harrison Cady's illustrations, plus exhibits focusing on his life work in conservation. A special treat for children is the live animal story times on Monday, Wednesday and Saturday mornings at 10.30am, July and August only. Outside is a little garden planted in the shape of a nosegay, and a 'touch and smell' plot of aromatic herbs.

Continue along Water Street to one of the oldest houses on Cape Cod. The ★ **Hoxie House** ❼, c1675 (open mid-June to mid-October, Monday to Saturday 10am–5pm, Sunday 1–5pm), has a classic salt box shape covered in dark shingles, with small rooms and tiny leaded windows. The restored interior is furnished with loans from the Boston Museum of Fine Arts.

Follow the shoreline of Shawme Pond back to the Town Hall and around to the far side to reach the **Old Town Cemetery** ❽ containing graves dating as far back as 1683. About 1 mile (1.6km) past the cemetery along Grove Street (you may want to return to your car at this point), at the intersection with Pine Street, is the ★★ **Heritage Plantation** ❾ (open mid-May to October, daily 10am–5pm, last admission 4.15pm), 76 acres (31 hectares). The principal attractions are the reproduction Shaker round barn which houses the plantation's collection of antique and vintage cars, the Art Museum featuring early American art, folk art and antique crafts, a 1912 working carousel, a military museum with a collection of hand-painted military miniatures, antique firearms, and Native American artifacts, and the extensive landscaped grounds.

From this point the tour continues by car. Head back to the center of town, turn onto Main Street, and make a left onto Jarvis Street. Cross Rt 6A, and then pass the railroad tracks and the depot for the **Cape Cod Scenic Railroad** ❿ (*see page 76*), turning left onto Factory Street. Turn left and first right to continue to the ★ **board-**

walk **⓫**, passing wide open marshland ringed by houses. The original boardwalk was swept away in a hurricane in 1991. The town pulled its resources together the following year to construct this 1,350-ft (412-meter) raised wooden walkway arching across Mill Creek and the salt marshes to the bay. Each wooden plank has been 'sponsored.' It is worth the walk to the beach for the wide view of Cape Cod Bay and the entrance to the canal.

Return to Jarvis Street and turn left onto Rt 6A. There is a **State Fishery ⓬** on the right about half a mile along 6A with viewing hours from 9am–3pm daily. Continue about 1¼ miles (2km) along Rt 6A to Spring Hill Road, the fourth left after Jarvis, to the **Wing Fort House ⓭** (open mid-June to August, Monday to Friday 10am–4pm). This c1641 colonial building is the country's oldest house continuously inhabited by the same family. The caretaker will give you a guided tour, pointing out its special details.

Quaker Meetinghouse

19

Follow Spring Hill Road as it curves around to the right, taking a sharp right onto Quaker Road and up a hill. At the top of this small hill is a ★ **Quaker Meetinghouse ⓮**. Built in 1810, it is the third meetinghouse on this site, but a congregation has been assembling here since 1657, making it the oldest Friends Meeting in the country.

Continue along Spring Hill Road and turn right on Rt 6A. Just past a large cranberry bog on the right, turn right onto Discovery Hill Road, following signs to ★★ **Green Briar Nature Center and Jam Kitchen ⓯** (open Monday to Saturday 10am–4pm, Sunday 1–4pm; in winter, tel: 888-6870 for information).This 57-acre (23-hectare) center is run by the Thornton W. Burgess society (*see page 17*), and is near the famous Briar Patch of Burgess's Peter Cottontail stories. Here you will find an informative nature center with trails, exhibits and natural history classes, and, if you follow your nose, Ida Putnam's jam kitchen. This kitchen has been making jams and preserves since 1903, and still uses turn-of-the-century methods and recipes today. In summer, the jams are placed in hot house windows where the heat of the sun slow cooks the fruit to perfection.

The tour now heads to Bourne, a residential town straddling the canal with strong military connections (the 21,000-acre/8,500-hectare Massachusetts Military Reservation on the Cape side and the Maritime Academy overlooking Buzzards Bay on the mainland side). Taking Rt 6A out of Sandwich in the direction of the bridge, after joining Rt 130 (Main Street), bear right onto Sandwich Rd. About ½ mile (0.8km) on the right is the **Pairpoint Glass Works** (open Monday to Saturday 9am–6pm, Sunday 10am–6pm, glass blowing demonstrations weekdays until 4.30pm), originally started in 1837 by Demming

At Green Briar Nature Center

The jam kitchen

Jarvis (of the Boston and Sandwich Glass Company) as a future prospect for his young son. The tradition of producing quality hand-made glass using formulas and methods from the 1800s continues today. Below the gift shop one can see the craftsmen at work.

Continue along Sandwich Road, passing underneath the Sagamore Bridge then following the bank of the ★ **Cape Cod Canal** and the railroad tracks. The need for a canal that would allow boats to avoid the dangerous shoals along the outer banks of Cape Cod was discussed as early as the late 1600s. It was not until July 29, 1914, however, that the canal was finally opened, narrowly beating the completion of the Panama Canal by 17 days. The Cape Cod Canal remains the widest sea-level canal in the world, at 480ft (146 meters). It is 17½ miles (28km) long, carrying 30,000 vessels a year. A bicycle path follows the length of the canal on both banks.

Aptuxet gift shop

For insight into the 'Cradle of American Commerce,' follow Sandwich Road past Rt 28 to a six-way intersection and turn right onto Perry Road which becomes Aptuxet Road a little further on. This will take you to a replica of the tiny ★ **Aptuxet Trading Post** (open May to mid-October, Tuesday to Saturday 10am–5pm and Sunday 2–5pm, closed Monday except July and August and long weekends, and open by appointment in spring and fall, tel: 759-9487). It was on this site that the first English-speaking trading post in North America was set up in 1627 to handle trade between Plymouth settlement, the Dutch in New York and the Wampanoag Indians.

Vertical Railroad Bridge

From the edge of the canal behind Aptuxet are views of the **Buzzards Bay Vertical Railroad Bridge** which spans the canal. The third longest bridge of this type in the world, it is 270ft (82 meters) high and 540ft (165 meters) long. The bridge is left in the raised position, and can be lowered within 2–3 minutes at the approach of a train. You stand a good chance of seeing this engineering feat in action at around 5 and 6pm, or contact the Army Corp of Engineers, who maintain the bridge, tel: 759-5991.

Soaking up the sunshine

Beaches and ponds: In Sandwich, **Town Neck Beach**, off Town Neck Road and Rt 6A, and **Sandy Neck Beach**, off Rt 6A near the Barnstable town line, are both on Cape Cod Bay. Two freshwater ponds are **Snake Pond** off Rt 130 and **Wakeby Pond** off Cotuit Road. Across the canal is **Scusset Beach Reservation**, with camping and trails. In Bourne, **Monument Beach** on Emmons Road off Shore Road, is on Buzzards Bay, with fairly warm water.

Conservation areas: the 742-acre (300-hecatre) **Shawme-Crowell State Forest** on Rt 130, in Sandwich, has trails and camp sites. **Red Brook Pond**, Thaxter Road, Cataumet, has 40 acres (16 hectares) of woodland.

Tour 2

Falmouth and Mashpee

West Falmouth – Quissett Harbor – Woods Hole – Falmouth Village – Mashpee *See map, p14–15*

This tour covers Falmouth, which straddles Buzzards Bay and Nantucket Sound, and has more shore and coastline than any other Cape town. Included is a visit to Woods Hole, site of the first landing on the Cape by Bartholomew Gosnold (1602), who gave the peninsula its permanent name, and Mashpee, home of the few remaining Native Americans in the area.

Bourne Farm

Starting near the end of Tour 1, take Rt 28A heading from Bourne to North Falmouth. This road takes you through lovely scenery, past cranberry bogs and many old houses. At the turn-off for Rt 28, 3½ miles (6km) past the border with Bourne, is **Bourne Farm** (open July to August, daily 2–4pm, or by appointment year round, tel: 548-0711), overlooking Crockers Pond. Built in 1775, this old farmstead is surrounded by a vegetable patch, wildflower garden, orchards and 40 acres (16 hectares) of land with trails.

21

Continuing on Rt 28A, you will reach **West Falmouth**. For a long time this village was mostly inhabited by Quakers and a Friends meetinghouse has been here almost since the founding of the town. The current **meetinghouse** (on Rt 28A, on the right before Blacksmith Shop Rd) was built in 1841, and the original stables for worshippers' horses still stands across the road. The surrounding cemetery has some early graves, unmarked as was the Quaker custom.

Rt 28A joins Rt 28. Continue until an intersection where Main Street turns left into Falmouth Center, and Locust Street continues straight. Take Locust Street, following signs to Woods Hole. Less than 2 miles (3km) further on, a right turn leads to lovely ★ **Quissett Harbor** (a worthwhile detour).

Quissett Harbor

Eel Pond, Water Street

Due to its naturally deep harbor and relatively unpolluted water, **Woods Hole** has been a center for marine research for well over a century, and since the 1930s has been home to three marine institutions of world renown. The first one you come to, on **Water Street**, is the headquarters of the **Woods Hole Oceanographic Institution** (WHOI), which has an exhibition center around the corner at 15 School Street (open Friday and Saturday 10am–4.30pm, Sunday noon–4:30pm). The tiny submarine the *Alvin*, famous for having located the wreck of the *Titanic* in 1986, is just one of the items on display. A little further along Water Street is the ★★ **Marine Biological Laboratory** (MBL) (tours June to September, Mon-

Nobska Light

day to Friday 1pm, tel: 548-3705, ext 423 for reservations), established in 1888 and specializing in the study of marine organisms as simple versions of more complex organisms, such as humans. It was research conducted on sea urchins which led to the breakthrough in in vitro fertilization. An excellent and very popular tour of the center is conducted by former researchers; reservations are required a week in advance in summer.

At the end of Water Street, turn right onto Albatross Street. Ahead on the left is the **National Marine Fisheries Service Aquarium** (NMFS) (open mid-June to mid-September, daily; mid-September to mid-June, Monday to Friday 10am–4pm), the first aquarium in the country when it opened in 1871. Upstairs are 'touch tank' tidal pools for kids to dip their hands into. Other exhibits include a lobster whose blue color defies a 20 million to 1 odds.

Bradley House

Backtrack along Water Street and turn left to visit the Woods Hole Historical Collection at the **Bradley House Museum** (573 Woods Hole Road, open mid-June to August, Tuesday to Saturday 10am–4pm) which includes a charming diorama of the town c1898. Housed in the barn outside are three old boats, a Spiritsail, a Herreshoff and a Cape Cod Knockabout, all of which have raced for the town, and a turn-of-the-century doctor's workshop.

Take Church Street to the most picturesque lighthouse on Cape Cod, ★★★ **Nobska Lighthouse**, on a high bluff, with Nobska Pond on the left of the road and the open shore of Nantucket Sound on the right. The original lighthouse was built in 1828, was rebuilt in 1876, and has been automated since 1985. From here, on a clear day, the view stretches to Martha's Vineyard and the Elizabeth Islands. Rounding Nobska Point, follow the shore and take the sixth left turn onto Oyster Pond Road, a couple of miles past the lighthouse. Shortly after this, take the right side

Spohr's Garden

of the fork onto Fells Road, at the end of which is

★ **Spohr's Garden** (open year round 7am–8pm), a 3-acre 1.2-hectare) garden leading down to a dock on the peaceful Oyster Pond. In May, 700,000 daffodils turn the garden into a sea of yellow.

Return to the shore and turn left where the road soon becomes a narrow spit of land wedged between salt marshes and the beach. This road was once the track for the railroad line between Falmouth and Woods Hole, and is now also the Shining Sea Bike Path, a popular 3⅗-mile (5.8-km) trail. On the right, along the beach, houses are built on stilts, a precautionary measure to avoid flooding during the hurricane season.

Turn left onto Shore Street, and left again onto Main Street to get to **Falmouth Village**, birthplace of Katherine Lee Bates, author of the lyrics for *America the Beautiful*. Park your car and walk west along Main Street, browsing in the many shops, inviting restaurants and cafes. The bustle dies out near the ★★★ **Village Green**, laid out in 1749 and surrounded by beautiful old houses, many of them built by wealthy sea captains. On the north side of the green stands a classic white New England church. **The First Congregational Church** was rebuilt in 1857 on the foundations of the 1796 original. Its bell was commissioned from Paul Revere, and is inscribed with these somber words: 'The living to the church I call, and to the grave I summon all.' Katherine Lee Bates's father served as minister here for a number of years.

Village Green and the First Congregational Church

Continue past the church and bear right at the end of the green onto Palmer Avenue. The Falmouth Historical Society runs museums in two adjacent houses here (both museums are open mid-June to mid-September, Monday to Friday 2–5pm). No 55 is the **Julia Wood House**, an elegant yellow federal-style house built in 1790. The original owner was Dr Francis Wicks, who was well known for his work in smallpox inoculations, and one room in the house is set up as a doctor's office of the period. Next door is the **Conant House**, and between the two buildings, a formal colonial garden. The Conant House, a late 18th-century half-Cape, was home to Reverend Samuel Palmer, minister of the First Congregational Church from 1730–75. Inside, one room is devoted to Katherine Lee Bates. Bates's birthplace stands on the opposite side of the green at 16 Main Street, where she lived until the age of 12.

Julia Wood House

From here you can take a detour either by foot (½ mile/0.8km beyond the Village Green) or by car to the **Highfield Theater**, once part of an estate owned by the two Beebe brothers. One of the mansions still stands, an impressive hulking semi-ruin. Behind this, the barn was converted into an equity theater in 1946 by New York producer Arthur Beckard. Although that venture did not last, in 1969 the College Light Opera Company was founded,

A closer look at shingle

Clue to the past

based on the idea of hiring university students from around the country as actors for the summer season. Each summer 32 actors and 17 musicians mount a different musical each week during the nine-week season.

Head now to **Mashpee**, following Main Street east out of town, as it turns into Rt 28. This is a very built up part of town, and the road is lined with shopping plazas and fast food restaurants. Turn off Rt 28 at the three-way fork with Sandwich and Locust Field Roads, taking the middle road, Sandwich, towards Mashpee. Continue to Rt 151 where you turn right, soon entering Mashpee.

Before the colonization of the Massachusetts Bay Colony, Indians of the Wampanoag Federation were thought to number about 40,000. Plague brought by white men wiped out many of them in 1617–18, and after the arrival of the *Mayflower* white settlers took over more and more Indian land. Richard Bourne, a missionary who spent much of his life trying to establish a Christian community among the Indians, was instrumental in securing about 16 sq miles (41.4 sq km) as the first Indian reservation in the United States, established in 1660. The Plantation, as it was called, had a population of about 500 Indians. There were scarcely 1,000 Indians left on Cape Cod by then and by the time of the Revolution this number had been halved.

Mashpee was incorporated as a town in 1870, and today there are about 600 descendants of the original Wampanoags. Much of the original land has been sold off, including 2,300 acres (930 hectares) bought up by the developers of the contentious New Seabury area, a development of shops, golf courses, restaurants, condos and houses along one of the prettiest parts of Mashpee's shoreline. The town is quiet, except on the Fourth of July weeknd when the annual Wampanoag Pow Wow attracts Native Americans from around the country.

The two main sites in Mashpee are both concerned with the history of the local Native Americans. From Rt 151, turn onto Rt 28 at the rotary, and shortly afterwards, turn left onto Meetinghouse Road. On the right is the **Old Indian Meetinghouse** (open June to August, Wednesday 10am–4pm and Friday 10am–3pm, rest of the year by appointment only, tel: 477-1536) built in 1684 and moved to its present location in 1717. This small simple building is the oldest standing church on Cape Cod, and one of the oldest in continual use in the USA, which is ironic, considering it was built in order to convert the local tribe from their pagan ways. The meetinghouse is still used by the Mashpee tribe for services and social activities.

Old Indian Meetinghouse

At the end of Meetinghouse Road turn left onto Rt 130, and ¼ mile (0.4km) further on the left is the **Mashpee Wampanoag Indian Museum** (open Wednesday to Saturday 10am–2pm, other times by appointment, tel: 477-536), a modest museum with several exhibits and much literature on the history of the local Indians.

Indian Museum

Beaches: In Falmouth, **Old Silver Beach**, on Buzzard's Bay off Rt 28A and Quaker Road, a good safe children's beach; **Surf Drive Beach**, on Nantucket Sound, located on Surf Drive; **Menauhant Beach**, on Nantucket Sound, off Rt 28 and Central Avenue, East Falmouth.

In Mashpee, **South Cape Beach State Park**, on Nantucket Sound, at the end of Great Neck Road, is a 2-mile (3-km) long barrier beach, which has a lifeguard, snack bar and rest rooms.

Ponds: Grews Pond, off Gifford Street at Goodwill Park in West Falmouth, with lifeguard. In Mashpee, **Mashpee** and **Wakeby Ponds**, off Rt 130, with good swimming; and **John's Pond**, off Loophole Road from Rt 151, with a snack bar, grills and picnic tables.

Conservation areas: In Falmouth, **Ashumet Holly and Wildlife Sanctuary** (closed Monday), Ashumet Road off Rt 151, East Falmouth, a bird sanctuary plus 65 varieties of holly in 45 acres (18 hectares) of land; **Waquoit Bay National Estuarine Research Reserve** (open year-round except during hunting season), off Rt 28 in East Falmouth, comprising 2,500 acres (1,011 hectares) of delicate estuaries and barrier beaches. In Mashpee, **Lowell Holly Reservation** (open May to October 10am–sunset), off Sandwich Road from Rt 130, comprising a Native American beech tree forest and over 500 holly trees; **South Mashpee Pine Barrens**, off Great Neck Road, with 300 acres (121 hectares) of rare pine barrens, Atlantic white cedar swamps and mixed forests.

Cartwheels on the sand

Tour 3

The County Seat

Barnstable Village – West Barnstable – Cotuit – Osterville – Hyannis *See map, p14–15*

This tour covers five of the seven villages that make up Barnstable, the largest town on the Cape and the County Seat, stretching from Cape Cod Bay in the north to Nantucket Sound in the south.

The oldest part of the town follows the coast along Barnstable Harbor. What first attracted early settlers was the abundance of salt hay for cattle feed. Incorporated in 1639 Barnstable's name probably came from a misspelling of the English town of Barnstaple. Reverend John Lothrop was the main driving force behind the initial settlement and it was under his guidance that the town flourished. During the 1800s, more than 800 ship captains lived here. Rt 6A is lined with many of their old houses.

Settlements along Nantucket Sound grew up toward the end of the 19th century and into the 20th. Centerville and Osterville are two of the wealthiest villages on the Cape. Cotuit is known locally as 'Little Harvard' because of the many academics who summer here. Hyannis, home to the Kennedys, is the commercial center of the Cape. Some 900,000 ferry passengers pass through here each summer on their way to and from the Islands.

County Courthouse
Near the town marina

This tour starts in **Barnstable Village** (the area on Rt 6A east of Rt 132). In the center of town, stands the impressive ★ **County Courthouse**, a large granite Greek Revival building constructed in 1834. Next to the courthouse stands the old wooden village hall, home to the **Barnstable Comedy Club**, the oldest amateur theater group in the country. Since 1922, it has been staging plays (not just comedies), with the involvement of local luminaries such as Kurt Vonnegut. Just east of the courthouse, turn left down Mill Way to see the pretty little **town marina** and the view across to Sandy Neck (*see page 29*).

Back on Rt 6A, turn left to arrive at the **Trayser Memorial Museum** (open mid-June to mid-October, Tuesday to Sunday, 1.30–4.30pm), originally the US Customs House. It now exhibits Native American artifacts, Victorian furnishings and children's toys and the carriage house in the back houses a horse-drawn hearse. A c1690s jail cell has also been moved here. Across the street is the **Unitarian Church**, designed by Guy Lowell in 1907, architect of the Boston Museum of Fine Arts.

A little further east along Rt 6A is the **Cape Cod Art Association** (open April to November, daily 10am–4pm

December to March, weekdays 10am–4pm) founded in 1948 to 'promote a high standard of fine art on Cape Cod.'

Back west along Rt 6A is ★ **Sturgis Library** (3090 Rt 6A, open Monday and Wednesday 10am–5pm, Tuesday and Thursday 1–5pm, 7–9pm, Friday 1–5pm). The oldest public library building in the country, it has an outstanding collection of genealogical records and a collection of books and maps that belonged to Cape Cod historian Henry Kittredge. Part of the library dates from 1644,when it was built for one of the town's founders, Reverend John Lothrop, by his parishioners. Across the street is the **Crocker Tavern**, built in the 1750s, and used as a meeting place for the Whigs during the Revolution.

Just past the library, on the corner of Rendezvous Lane, is the white clapboard **Olde Colonial Courthouse**, used originally for the Kings Court. In September 1774, a band of patriots entered the building and forced the King's Court sessions to end. Today, the building is used by Tales of Cape Cod, an organization founded in 1949 to collect and preserve Cape Cod's oral history and folklore (tel: 362-6636 for information).

Olde Colonial Courthouse

Across the street from the courthouse is St Mary's Episcopal Church, where you will find tranquil, English-style ★ **gardens**. Half a mile (0.8km) further along Rt 6A is the old **Lothrop Hill Cemetery**, the final resting place of many of the founders of Barnstable, including John Lothrop. The earliest grave dates from 1648.

In St Mary's gardens

Those with a keen interest in the history of Cape Cod may want to take a detour to the **William Brewster Nickerson Memorial Room** (open Monday, Wednesday and Friday 8.30am–4pm, Tuesday 8.30am–3pm). Located in the library of the Cape Cod Community College, on Rt 132, it houses an extensive collection detailing the lives of the people of Cape Cod and the Islands.

Return to Rt 6A, and continue westward, past views of the salt marshes. In West Barnstable, turn left onto Rt 149 (Meetinghouse Way). About 1 mile (2km) further on stands the old ★★★ **West Parish Meetinghouse**. In 1616, a band of dissenters from the Church of England met secretly in London and organized the first Congregational Church. Fleeing England in 1634, the group, headed by John Lothrop, settled in Barnstable in 1639, and the first meetinghouse was built in 1646. It is a magnificent example of early colonial architecture; inside is a Paul Revere half-ton bell cast in 1806.

Rt 149 now heads south, through Marston Mills. At the intersection with Rt 28, bare right towards Santuit; just before the intersection with Rt 130 is the ★ **Cahoon Museum of American Art** (open April to January, Tuesday to Saturday 10am–4pm), in the former home of artists Ralph and Martha Cahoon. This museum covers Ameri-

27

West Parish Meetinghouse

Cahoon detail

Sampling the penny candy

Crosby Yacht Yard

can art from pre-Revolutionary times to the present, with changing displays showing the work of early itinerant portrait painters, the Hudson River School of landscape painting, maritime paintings and American impressionists.

Take the road directly opposite the museum, Main Street, which passes through Santuit to **Cotuit**, famous the world over for its oysters. Main Street has some lovely old homes. On the left, just past Oakwood Street, is the **Samuel Dotteridge Homestead** (1148 Main Street, open mid-June to August, Thursday to Sunday 2.30–5pm, September to October, Saturday 2.30–5pm), built in 1790 and the home of a carpenter and his family for the first half of the 19th century. It is authentically furnished to reflect the circumstances of a fairly poor craftsman of the time.

Heading back along Main Street, turn right onto Old Shore Road and follow the coast along Putnam and then Old Post Roads to Rt 28. Turn right here, bear right at the fork with Rt 149, and then right to **Osterville**. On the left before Osterville's center is a little red building with a white porch, the ★ **Country Store** (877 Main Street, open daily 7:30am–8:30pm), run by the same family since 1915. Inside are jars of penny candy and the narrow aisles and nooks and crannies of a genuine general store.

Before exploring the many shops of Main Street, visit three interesting buildings (open June to September, Tuesday, Thursday and Sunday 1.30–4.30pm). At the corner of West Bay Road stands the ★ **Captain John Parker House**, an early 19th-century home containing a collection of spoils from the China trade and a toy display upstairs. Outside is a pretty period garden and next to this the **Cammett House**, c1728, a 'one pile deep narrow house', with just one long room. Also on this property is the ★ **Crosby Boat Shop**, containing old models of the wooden catboat designed by Herbert Crosby in the mid 1800s. Used as a fishing boat until the turn of the century, the catboat became popular among pleasure boat skippers including John F. Kennedy. The Crosbys are still building boats and their yacht yard is on Crosby Lane nearby.

Continue down Parker Road and turn left onto Sea View Avenue to see some prime Osterville property. Homes on the shore side of the road overlook Nantucket Sound and have open beach as their backyards. Now head east on Main Street towards **Centerville**. At Craigville Beach Road, take a left onto what becomes Main Street in Centerville. The ★ **Centerville Historical Society Museum** (open mid-June to mid-September, Wednesday to Sunday 1.30–4.30pm) is just ahead. Among the exhibits in the 14 rooms of this 1840s house are over 300 quilts and a costume collection spanning 300 years.

Heading back south along Main Street, the road curves left and follows Craigville Beach before heading to Hyannis is. About 1½ miles (2.4 km) from Craigville Beach bear left onto Smith Street (not towards Hyannisport). (Hyannisport is, by the way, the location of the Kennedy Compound, but there is nothing to see since high fences guard it from public view. The only way of catching a glimpse is to take one of the harbor cruises.)

At the end of Smith Street take a right onto Greenwood Avenue and first left onto Ocean Avenue. Bear right onto Gosnold Street which heads directly to the **Kennedy Memorial**, at Veterans Beach. The memorial is appropriately inscribed: 'I believe it is important that this country sail and not lie still in the harbor.'

Turning right out of the memorial site, follow the edge of the water, past busy Hyannis Harbor from where ferries leave for the Islands. At the lights turn left onto Main Street. The **John F. Kennedy Hyannis Museum** (open in summer, Monday to Saturday 10am–4pm, Sunday 1–4pm; in winter, Wednesday to Saturday 10am–4pm), housed in the Old Town Hall, was set up in 1992 to satisfy the hoards of visitors in search of something of the Kennedys. The exhibits mostly consist of old photographs of the Kennedy family taken around Hyannisport and a video narrated by Walter Cronkite. Not far away, on High School Street, is **St Xavier Church**, where, for years, the Kennedy clan have come to worship; the Kennedy brothers, Joseph, John and Robert were all altar boys at the church. John F. Kennedy and his family worshipped here before and during his presidency, and a plaque marks their usual pew.

This way for the ferry

JFK at the helm

29

Beaches and ponds: Sandy Neck Beach, on Cape Cod Bay off Rt 6A in West Barnstable, a beautiful 6-mile (10-km) barrier beach with rest rooms and snack bar; in Centerville, **Craigville Beach**, Craigville Beach Road, on Nantucket Sound, with rest rooms and outdoor showers, and **Long Beach**, at the western end of Craigville Beach can be reached on foot from Craigville). In Hyannis, **Kalmus Park Beach**, at the end of Ocean Street, good for windsurfing; **Veterans Beach**, good for children, with bath house, grills and picnic tables; **Sea Street Beach** (also called Orrin Keyes Beach), with rest rooms and a bath house. For fresh-water swimming there is **Hathaway Pond**, Phinney's Lane, Barnstable Village, with lifeguard and bath house.

Conservation areas: Sandy Neck Great Salt Marsh Conservation Area, off Sandy Neck Road in West Barnstable, the East Coast's largest remaining salt marsh, with a 9-mile (15-km) round trip trail; **West Barnstable Conservation Area**, Popple Bottom Road off Rt 149 near Rt 6, with wooded trails; **Cape Cod Horticultural Society Park**, Rt 28 near East Bay Road, Osterville, with walkways through wetlands and wooded areas.

Tour 4

The Mid-Cape

Yarmouthport – South Yarmouth – South Dennis – Dennis Village

The first settlers in Yarmouth were led by *Mayflower* passenger Stephen Hopkins in 1638. The town was incorporated the following year, probably named after the English port of Great Yarmouth. However, there are claims that over 1,000 years before this the Bass River was explored by a group of Vikings led by Leif Eriksson.

Yarmouthport in the north was once home to many sea captains, and it was from here that packet boats sailed to Boston, and whalers set out on their long journeys. There are more beautiful old homes lining this section of Rt 6A (once called Captain's Row) than along any other section on the Cape. South Yarmouth, along the Bass River, was settled by Quakers at the turn of the 19th century, and many of their lovely houses remain.

Yarmouthport B&B

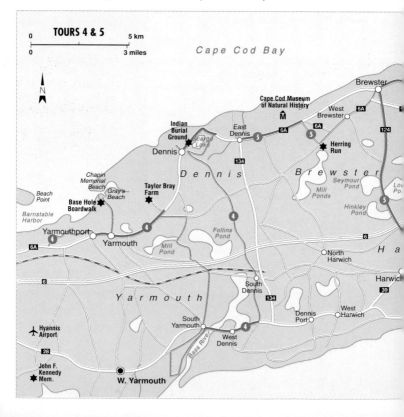

TOURS 4 & 5

0   5 km
0   3 miles

N

Cape Cod Bay

Brewster

Cape Cod Museum
of Natural History
Ⓜ

West
Brewster   6A

6A

Indian
Burial
Ground   East
Dennis

Scargo
Lake

6A

124

Herring
Run

Dennis

B r e w s t e r

Chapin
Memorial
Beach

Gray's
Beach

Taylor Bray
Farm

134

D e n n i s

Seymour
Pond

Lo
Po

Beach
Point

Base Hole
Boardwalk

Mill
Ponds

Hinkley
Pond

Barnstable
Harbor

Yarmouthport

6A

Yarmouth

Follins
Pond

6

North
Harwich

H a

Mill
Pond

6

Y a r m o u t h

South
Dennis

134

Harwic

39

Hyannis
Airport

South
Yarmouth

Dennis
Port

West
Harwich

28

West
Dennis

Bass River

John F.
Kennedy
Mem.

W. Yarmouth

from Rt 6 in Barnstable, take the turn-off at Willow Street towards Yarmouthport and turn right onto Rt 6A. This brings you into the center of **Yarmouthport**. ★ **Hallet's General Store** (139 Rt 6A, open in summer, daily 8am–9pm, in winter, daily 8am–5pm), on the right a little way along, started out as a drug store in 1889, and has been run by the same family ever since. Thacher Taylor Hallet, the first owner, served as pharmacist, postmaster, selectman and justice of the peace, and upstairs is an informal museum documenting Yarmouth's history through one family's eyes.

Park in the lot next to the post office on the right, and walk towards the Village Green ahead. On the left is the magnificent ★★ **Winslow Crocker House** (250 Main Street, open June 1 to October 15, Tuesday, Thursday, Saturday and Sunday noon–5pm). Now run by the Society for the Preservation of New England Antiquities, this c1780s Georgian house is rich with interior paneling, detail and antiques.

Just ahead is the ★ **Village Green** enclosed by a picket fence. Across from the green stands the **New Church**,

Village Green
New Church

31

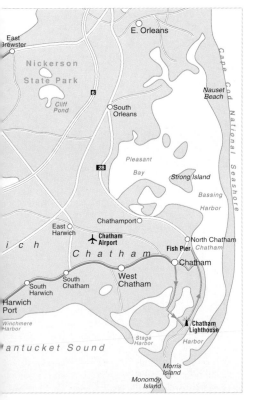

Bangs Hallet House

Boardwalk across Clay's Creek

Friends Meetinghouse

or Swedenborgian Church, named after the Swedish sci
entist-philosopher of the same name. This church became
the most influential in Yarmouth during the second half of
the 19th century. It has one of the finest organs in the coun
try, reflecting the church's emphasis on 'worship in the
sphere of great music.'

On the western side of the green stands the ★ **Captain
Bangs Hallet House** (open June and September, Sunday
1–4pm, July and August, Thursday, Friday and Sunday
1–4pm), the home of a prosperous sea captain and his wife
in the late 1800s. Be sure to see the original 1740 kitchen.
The Historical Society, which runs the house, also main
tains a 2-mile (3.2-km) nature trail starting at the gate
house (the entrance is behind the post office) and lead
ing to the tiny **Kelly Chapel**, built in 1873 by a Quaker
for a daughter who was grieving for the loss of her young
son. The chapel was moved here from its original location
in South Yarmouth.

When you have returned to your car, you may want to
take a short scenic detour onto Thacher Shore Road. All
along here, amongst the marshes and old houses, is a real
sense of old Cape Cod. At Wharf Lane, bare right and
curve to the left onto Water Street which leads over a small
bridge across Mill Creek and eventually back to Rt 6A.
Go through Yarmouthport again and about ½ mile (0.8km)
past the village green, turn left onto Center Street which
ends at Gray's Beach. From here, the raised wooden **Bass
Hole Boardwalk** extends across Clay's Creek and open
marshland. Although Bass Hole is now silted up, it was
from here that the Bray Brothers operated a successful
shipyard in the mid-1700s.

Backtrack on Rt 6A, and take the third road on the right,
a very sharp turn onto Setucket Road. Turn right again onto
North Dennis Road which wanders past two pretty ponds,
Mill and Follins. After the overpass, bear right to **South
Yarmouth**. Shortly before the intersection with Rt 28
stands the ★ **Friends Meetinghouse and Cemetery**.
South Yarmouth, originally called Friends Village, was
settled at the end of the 1600s by Quakers fleeing perse
cution in other towns. Inside the church, a partition which
can be lowered to divide the sexes still uses the original
rope and log operation.

Although a rather unattractive section of Rt 28 cuts
across Main Street, over the Bass River Bridge and on
to Dennis, the area between North Main/Old Main street
and Kelly Road and Pleasant Street enclose what was once
the old ★★ **Quaker Village**, also called Bass River Vil
lage, whose houses span most of the styles popular on Cape
Cod in the 1800s. Continue down Pleasant Street to a three-
way intersection with River Street, which is said to be
the first traffic rotary in the United States. On River Street

the **Judah Baker Windmill**, built in 1791, has been moved to various locations between Dennis and Yarmouth during its 100 working years. It was common practice to buy and sell windmills, and have them 'dismasted' and moved when required.

The **Bass River**, the border between Yarmouth and Dennis, is the largest tidal river in New England. It is claimed that the Viking Leif Eriksson explored this area over 1,000 years ago and built a camp 5 miles (8km) up river at Blue Rock Heights. This has never been proven, but many street names have a Viking ring to them in honor of the legend.

We now head to **Dennis**, part of Yarmouth until 1793. Roads leading off Rt 6A lead to the early settlements of Quivett Neck and Sesuit Harbor, where a fishing industry once flourished. It was near here that the first cranberry bogs were cultivated by Henry Hall in 1807, although before sugar was readily available to sweeten the tart berries not much was made of the crop.

A local idiosyncrasy has put South Dennis, where this tour now heads, due north of Dennisport and West Dennis. Follow Rt 28 across the Bass River Bridge. Bear left onto Old Main Street to enter the 'South Dennis Historic District.' On the corner of Trotting Park Road and Old Main Street stands **Jericho House** (open July to August, Wednesday and Friday 2–4pm), a shingled full Cape built in 1801 and housing a fine collection of 19th-century antiques. Behind the house is the **barn**, built in 1810, containing farming tools, a model saltworks and a race cart from the days when sea captains spent their days on land racing horses, plus a wonderful ★ '**driftwood zoo**' carved from flotsam by Sherman Woodward in the 1950s.

South Parish Church

Head north on Main Street and you will shortly come to the fine ★★ **South Parish Congregational Church** (234 Main Street), famous for its chandelier made of Sandwich glass, and Sneltzer organ, reputed to be the oldest pipe organ in continual use in the USA. Main Street meanders north through this old section of town, passing many handsome houses and, on the left, ½ mile (0.8km) from the church, the gingerbread-style **Free South Dennis Library**. After crossing Rt 6, Main becomes Old Bass River Road. Just before the intersection with Rt 6A, make a sharp right turn onto Scargo Hill Road to **Scargo Hill Tower**. The 28-ft (8.5-meter) tower offers ★ **views** across the width of the Cape and on a clear day all the way to Provincetown. Scargo Lake is a deep glacial kettle pond with good swimming and fishing.

Continue on Scargo Hill Road, and take a sharp left turn onto Main Street. Past Seaside Avenue look for a sign to the **Burial Ground of the Nobscusset Tribe of Indians**.

To the Indian Burial Ground

Enclosed by an old iron fence, this quiet spot has only a few trees to mark the final resting place of the Indians of this area.

Main Street follows the shore of Scargo Lake into the center of Dennis. Before the post office on the left is the

Cape Cinema

Cape Cinema (tel: 385-4477 for information) in an arts complex that includes the Cape Playhouse and the Cape Museum of Fine Arts. It was in this cinema that the world premier of *The Wizard of Oz* was shown in 1930. Inside is a splendid art deco ★★ **mural**, the largest single ceiling mural in the country, painted by Rockwell Kent and Jo Mielziner and depicting the heavenly bodies, filled with constellations and comets. The **Cape Playhouse** (box office, tel: 385-3911) housed in a former 19th-century Unitarian Meetinghouse, is home to America's oldest continuously operating professional summer theater and has launched the careers of many future stars (*see page 62*). The **Cape Museum of Fine Arts** (open Tuesday to Saturday, 10am–5pm, Sunday 1–5pm) exhibits work of some of the Cape's most important artists.

Just past the town's bandstand, turn right onto Nobscusset Road, to visit the **Rev. Josiah Dennis Manse**, home of the man for whom the town was named. Inside rooms are furnished as they would have been in his day. Behind the Manse is a 1770 one-room **school house** moved to this location in the 1970s. Inside are wrought-iron desks and wood paneling.

Dennis Manse

Beaches: Seagull Beach, off South Sea Avenue from Rt 28, West Yarmouth, a long sandy beach on Nantucket Sound; **Gray's Beach**, Center Street off Rt 6A. In Dennis Village, **Chapin Memorial Beach**, Chapin Beach Road west of Dennis Village, a long beach lined with dunes; **Corporation Beach**, Corporation Road, with concession stands and backed by dunes; **Mayflower Beach**, off Beach Street; **West Dennis Beach**, off Davis Beach Road, on Nantucket Sound, with lifeguards.

Beach babe

Ponds: Flax Pond, off North Main Street, South Yarmouth, with lifeguard and picnic area; **Swan Pond Overlook**, off Center Street from Searsville Road and Rt 134, Dennisport, with beach and picnic area; **Scargo Lake** (*see page 33*), two beaches (one with access from Rt 6A, and one from Scargo Hill Road), with good swimming.

Conservation areas: Botanical trails of the Historical Society of Old Yarmouth (*see page 32*); **Taylor-Bray Farm** on Taylor-Bray Farm Road off Rt 6A, Yarmouthport, with a working farm, picnic area and nature trails; **Indian Lands Conservation Area**, with a 2-mile (3.2-km) walk along the Bass River in South Yarmouth; **Fresh Pond Conservation Area**, off Rt 134 in Dennisport, with trails, picnic areas and a boating area for small sailboats.

Tour 5

Captains and Cranberries

Brewster – Harwich – Chatham *See map, p30–1*

Brewster is famous for its gracious captains' houses. Ninety-nine deepwater captains lived here between 1780 and 1870, a higher percentage of the population than in any other town in America. The town was settled as early as 1659, but was originally the North Parish of Harwich. The North and South parishes of Harwich were for a long time at odds with each other, primarily because the South was mainly agricultural and therefore poorer than the North with its wealthy captains. In 1803, the North Parish incorporated itself as a separate town, taking the name of a *Mayflower* passenger, Elder William Brewster.

From the end of Tour 4 in Dennis, head east on Rt 6A to reach the Brewster–Dennis border. About 2 miles (3.2km) further on the road passes a late 18th-century **wooden windmill**. Behind the windmill is the tiny **Harris-Black House**, a one-room half-Cape house built around 1795 to house a family of 12. (Both sites are open July to August, Tuesday to Friday 1–4pm.)

Continue on 6A towards **Brewster**. Within ½ mile (0.8km) on the left is the ★★ **Cape Cod Museum of Natural History** (open year round, Monday to Saturday 9:30am–4:30pm and Sunday 12:30–4:30pm), covering 82 acres (33 hectares) of coastal land and especially appealing to children. Take the first right after the museum onto Paines Creek Road and turn right at the T-junction onto Stoney Brook Road. Up a hill, on the left, is the ★★ **Stoney Brook Herring Run** and the **Stoney Brook Grist Mill** (open May to June, Thursday to Saturday 2–5pm and July

Catch as catch can at the Stoney Brook Herring Run

35

At the Museum of Natural History

Fun for the young

Brewster Store
First Parish Church

to August, Friday only 2–5pm). At the end of April or the beginning of May, over half a million alewives (fresh-water-born herring that live in the sea) migrate up Stoney Brook to the mill ponds to spawn, each female laying up to 100,000 eggs. The herring run flows alongside an area known as Factory Village in the 19th century. The present grist mill (museum) is the only surviving remnant of this once booming area.

Head back along Stoney Brook Road to Rt 6A and turn right towards Brewster Center. A little further on is the ★ **New England Fire and History Museum** (1429 Rt 6A, open mid-May to mid-September, Monday to Friday 10am–4pm, Saturday to Sunday noon–4pm, mid-September to Columbus Day, Saturday and Sunday noon–4pm). Historic fire engines (more that 30 of them still working) are a big hit with children. Also here is a re-production smithy and an apothecary shop.

From here Rt 6A is lined with sea captains' houses, most of which now house antique shops and guest houses. Half a mile (1km) further on is the old **town hall**, c1881, built in a Queen Anne style. Across the street further on is the picturesque **Brewster Ladies Library**, established in 1852 by a group of public-spirited Brewster women.

At the intersection of Rt 6A and Rt 137 is the **Brewster Store** (open winter, daily 6:30am–5pm, spring and autumn, daily 6am–6pm, summer 6am–10pm). Built in 1852 as a Universalist Church, the building was sold for just $1 in 1886 to William Knowles who turned it into a general store. It still retains the atmosphere of an old-fashioned general store, though its merchandise is now geared to tourists, who flood through its doors in summer.

Past the Brewster store, on the left, is the ★★★ **First Parish Church**, a beautifully proportioned white clapboard church, with a light airy interior of clean lines and

pointed windows. Established as the Congregational Church in 1700, this building, called the Church of Captains, was erected in 1834 as the third meetinghouse on this site. An early town cemetery is located behind the church with graves of church elders, Revolutionary soldiers and sea captains.

About 2½ miles (4km) further along on the left is the **Brewster Historical Museum** (3341 Rt 6A, open May to June and September to October, Saturday to Sunday 1–4pm, July to August, Tuesday to Friday 1–4pm), housed in an 1840 homestead. Displays include the old East Brewster Post Office, a c1884 barbershop, memorabilia from Brewster shipmaster days, dolls and toys. From here the Spruce Hill Trail follows an old carriage road on a 15-minute walk to Cape Cod Bay and a small sandy beach.

Head back towards Brewster Center and turn left onto Route 124 towards Harwich. If you have children, you may want to turn left onto Tubman Road, about ¾ mile (1.2km) further on, for **Bassett Wild Animal Farm** (620 Tubman Road, open mid-May to mid-September, daily 10am–5pm), a mini-zoo with an enclosed animal petting area, pony rides, and a range of domestic and exotic birds and animals.

Out and about in Brewster

37

Rt 124 will take you into **Harwich**, past Seymour and Hinkly ponds on the right and Long Pond on the left, followed by cranberry bogs. Old Harwich, incorporated in 1694, has resisted the kind of over-development that has plagued other towns on the Cape. Harwich's Winchmere Harbor (*see page 38*) is one of the prettiest on Cape Cod.

It was in Harwich that the first commercial cultivation of cranberries began in the 1840s and the town is still a leader in Cape cranberry production. Berries range in color from purple during the winter to green in summer and maroon in autumn. During the harvest in October the bright red berries are shaken from the bushes and the bogs flooded, so that the berries rise to the surface.

★ **Harwich Village center** is a pleasant surprise after the new housing developments along Route 124. It retains its old New England village feel, with small roads lined with old houses, picket fences and large shade trees. At the intersection of Route 124 and Main Street, on the right is the **First Congregational Church**, established in 1747. This lovely white building with delicate detailing is the third built on the site. The 100-ft (30-meter) steeple was added in 1854.

Congregational Church

Diagonally across from the church is the white-columned ★ **Brooks Academy Museum** (open June to September, Thursday to Sunday 1–4pm), containing Indian artifacts, old photographs and diaries of Harwich residents of old, and exhibits of the history and culture of

Cranberry harvest

the cranberry bog industry. Behind the museum is the **Old Powder House**, used to store ammunition during the Revolutionary War. It is hard to imagine that this tiny building held enough ammunition to defend the entire town in case of attack.

On Main Street, turn right opposite the Town Hall onto Bank Street, which will take you past more old houses and cranberry bogs to Rt 28. A left turn will take you towards ★★ **Winchmere Harbor** and then on to Chatham. Originally a salt-water pond, the harbor was first developed at the end of the Civil War when several retired sea captains laid out a race track around the pond. In 1899, after the sea had broken into the pond, the town decided it was more suitable for a fishing fleet than a fleet of racehorses and it became Winchmere Harbor.

Winchmere Harbor

Chatham's history of European involvement began in 1606 when Samuel de Champlain, looking for a more hospitable land than Nova Scotia, tried to land at Stage Harbor but was fought off by Indians. In 1656, under more friendly circumstances, the sachem Mattaquason sold what is now Chatham to a Yarmouth man, William Nickerson, and the area was settled by his family and other *Mayflower* descendants. Originally called Monomoy, the town was incorporated in 1712, and named after the Kentish river port of Chatham in England.

One of the most significant events in recent history was the now famous Chatham Break. A particularly ferocious storm in January 1987 created a breach in the barrier beach which had previously protected Chatham harbor and some prime waterside properties. More than a dozen houses were destroyed. A good view of the Break is visible from Chatham Light (*see page 39*). Chatham remains a cohesive town; its center is lined with charming shops, and along the shore are well-kept shingled cottages and elegant stately homes.

A left at the rotary and a left again onto Depot Road brings you to the ★★ **Chatham Railroad Museum** (open mid-June to mid-September, Tuesday to Saturday 10am–4pm). This delightful Victorian gingerbread depot, painted yellow with red trim, served as Chatham's railroad station from 1887–1937. In its heyday, over 22,000 passengers used this line annually. On view is a 75-year-old caboose from the New York Central System, exhibits of photos and equipment relating to the Cape's railroad history.

Take a right back onto Rt 28, cross over the rotary, continue straight onto Stage Harbor Road. Near the town landing at **Stage Harbor** at the end of the road is the site where Samuel de Champlain landed in 1606. Also near here is the burial site of Squanto, an indispensable friend to the early Plymouth settlement. He must have been a man capable of great forgiveness, since he was one of 24 Indians kidnapped by Captain Thomas Hunt in 1614 and sold as slaves in Spain. He escaped, sought the protection of a merchant in England and eventually returned to his homeland, where he acted as interpreter between the Pilgrims and the sachem Massasoit, and taught the settlers how to survive in their new land.

The ★ **Old Atwood House Museum** (open mid-June to September, Tuesday to Friday 1–4pm) is back up Stage Harbor Road just past Bridge Road. The house dates from 1752, and displays memorabilia, furniture and clothing. Downstairs are exhibits explaining the workings of the local industries of cranberry production and salt works. The ★ **Mural Barn** in the back houses a set of murals painted by Alice Wight in the 1930s and 1940s. These paintings caused quite a stir at the time for their portrayal of local Chatham people in scenes from the New Testament. Christ is represented as a local fisherman preaching to the multitudes from the prow of his dory.

Bridge Street, left out of the museum parking lot, will take you over a drawbridge to Main Street (left at the T-junction) leading to ★★ **Chatham Light and Coast Guard Station**. In 1808 two lighthouses were built on this site, to distinguish them from the single Highland Light in Truro. By 1923 a system had been developed to distinguish between different lighthouses by the rotation of their lights instead of the number of lighthouses on a site, so one of Chatham's twin lights was moved to Nauset Light Beach in Eastham (*see page 44*). This dramatic spot is loved by visitors and residents alike. From here one can see the famous Chatham Break (*see page 38*)

Main Street changes names a couple of times but will still take you to the ★★ **Fish Pier**. Here you can watch the Chatham fishermen unload their day's catch in the

Chatham Railroad Museum

39

Alice Wight's Christ

Chatham Light

Prize catch

afternoon. Fishing is still an important town industry supplying markets in New York, New Bedford, and Boston as well as locally.

On Friday evenings (from 8pm) in summer the place to be is the **Kate Gould Park**, on the right side of Main Street in the center of town. This is where the Chatham Band entertains crowds of up to 6,000 with waltzes, big band numbers and spontaneous singalongs.

Beaches: Eight public beaches located off Rt 6A in Brewster, the nicest of which is **Paine's Creek Beach**, Paine's Creek Road; **Red River Beach**, off Depot Road or Uncle Venies Road from Rt 28 in Harwich, with parking for day visitors (there is also a free trolley service which operates in Harwich, making the beaches which are restricted to town sticker-holders accessible to everyone); in Chatham, **Hardings Beach**, Hardings Beach Road off Barn Hill Road from Rt 28; **Ridgevale Beach**, Ridgevale Road from Rt 28; **Cockle Cove Beach**, Cockle Cove Road off Rt 28, a good choice for families with small children; and **Chatham Light Beach**, below the Chatham Light parking area (stairs to the beach).

On the beach

Ponds: Long Pond and **Sheep Pond**, both off of Rt 124, Brewster; in Harwich, **Hinkleys** and **Seymour Ponds**, off Rt 124, **Bucks Pond**, off Rt 39, and **Pleasant Bay**, off Rt 28; in Chatham, **Schoolhouse Pond**, School House Road off Sam Ryders Road and **Oyster Pond**, (salt water) off Stage Harbor Road.

Conservation areas: In Brewster, **Nickerson State Park** (open daily 8am–8pm) entrance on Rt 6A just past Crosby Lane, including 8 miles (12km) of bike paths, eight kettle ponds, and 420 camp sites; **Punkhorn Parklands**, Run Hill Road off Stoney Brook Road, with 45 miles (72km) of trails through forests, meadows and marshes; **Spruce Hill Conservation Area**, behind the Brewster Historical Museum (*see page 37*). In Harwich, **Thompson's Field**, south of Rt 39 near Chatham Road, a 93-acre (37-hectare) preserve; **Bell's Neck Conservation Area**, off Bell's Neck Road from Depot Road, or North Road from Rt 28 in West Harwich, comprising tidal creeks and marshland ideal for canoeing and bird watching. In Chatham, the **Monomoy National Wildlife Refuge**, off Morris Island Road (open daily dawn to dusk), is considered to be one of the four remaining 'wilderness' areas between Maine and New Jersey. Every species of bird native to New England can be found here, 285 in all, and the animal inhabitants include thousands of harbor seals and some rare gray seals who spend the winter here. Guided tours are available from the **Cape Cod Museum of Natural History** (tel: 896-3867) or the **Wellfleet Bay Wildlife Sanctuary** (tel: 349-2615).

Tour 6

Orleans and Eastham

Rock Harbor – Meetinghouse Museum – Nauset Beach – Nauset Light – Three Sisters Lights

Orleans is the only town on Cape Cod without an English or Indian name. Settled in 1644, and originally part of Eastham, the town was incorporated in 1797. Although no record exists explaining the choice of name, a popular theory is that it was named after the Duke de Orleans of France, Louis-Phillipe de Bourbon, who visited the area that year during his exile. Orleans came under fire from a German U-boat in 1918, making it the only place in the continental USA to suffer from enemy fire in either World War. Unfortunately the incident happened on a Sunday when the pilots and crewmen stationed nearby at the Chatham air base were all in Provincetown attending a ball game; retaliation was therefore not as vigorous as it might have been

Jonathan Young Windmill

Orleans now serves as the year-round commercial center for the Lower Cape, and Rts 6A and 28 are very built up. But turn off these main roads onto any small road and you will discover the charming houses, shaded lanes and well-tended gardens of old Orleans.

41

Just south of the rotary at the intersection of Rts 6A and 6 is the **Jonathan Young Windmill**, c1720s (open July to August, daily 11am–4pm), on the edge of Town Cove. Built in South Orleans, the windmill was given to the town in 1983. During restoration a large portion of the early mill machinery was found to be intact. The mill has interpretative displays.

Continuing on Rt 6A, bear left onto Rt 28 and less than ½ mile (1km) further, on the left, is the **French Cable Station Museum** (41 Rt 28, open July to August, Tuesday to Saturday 2–4pm). From 1880 to 1940, this office was a key link in communications between America and Europe. The first transatlantic

Rock Harbor

Nauset Beach

Cove Burying Ground

cable, established in 1879, ran underwater from Brest, France, to St Pierre Island off Newfoundland and on to Nauset Beach. In 1890, the station was moved to this location and in 1898, a direct cable was laid from Brest to the nearby Town Cove. Decommissioned in 1959, the building was bought in 1971 by nine former French Telegraph Cable Co employees who set up the museum.

Just past the museum, turn right onto Main Street which becomes Rock Harbor Road. At the end here is ★★ **Rock Harbor**, one of the prettiest in New England, with a small beach and marshland nearby. This was the site of one of the few battles of the War of 1812 to take place on Cape Cod soil. On December 19, 1814, the local Orleans militia repulsed the British *HMS Newcastle*. After the war until the mid-1800s, this harbor was the center of town, a bustling area full of shops, small factories and the landing spot for packet boats to Boston.

Return by way of Rock Harbor Road and Main Street to the center of Orleans. About ¾ mile (1.2km) along Main Street is the ★ **Meetinghouse Museum** (open July to September, Tuesday and Wednesday 10am–noon), home of the Orleans Historical Society. Built in 1833 as the Universalist Meetinghouse in a pure Greek Revival style, this former church is a good example of the architecture of the period. Inside are Indian arrowheads, marine artifacts, farm implements and ammunition shells from the War of 1812.

A little further along, Main Street turns into Beach Road leading to ★★★ **Nauset Beach**, one of the main reasons for Orleans' popularity – a 9-mile (15-km) stretch of sand dunes and surf belonging to the National Seashore.

Return to the Rotary on Rt 6 where the tour began, heading towards Provincetown, and you will be on the town line with **Eastham**, where Myles Standish and his scouting party from the *Mayflower* had their first meeting with the Native Americans, at what is now known as First Encounter Beach (*see page 43*). Eastham, originally called Nauset, was later settled in 1644 by Plymouth inhabitants. In the late 1600s Eastham rivaled Plymouth in political importance. It is now a very quiet town, with no real town center, but with the National Seashore owning a third of the land, there is plenty to do and see.

About 1¼ miles (2km) along Rt 6 from the town boundary with Orleans is the ★ **Cove Burying Ground** containing three unmarked graves of *Mayflower* passengers plus lovely old gravestones dating from the end of the 17th and beginning of the 18th centuries.

About ¾ mile (1.2km) further, just before the Visitors Information Center, turn right at the sign for the Fort Hill Area, on Fort Hill Road. This takes you to the ★ **Captain Edward Penniman House**, an elegant French Sec-

Capt Edward Penniman House

ond-Empire style house. Captain Penniman left Eastham in 1842 at the age of 11 to seek his fortune. By the age of 29 he was master of his own whaling bark, and built this house in 1867, the most expensive in town at the time. Mrs Penniman and their three children accompanied the captain on several whaling trips, journeys sometimes lasting up to four years. Published accounts of Mrs Penniman's journals from these voyages are on sale from the National Seashore visitors centers. Past the house is the Fort Hill Nature Area with marked trails and a beach.

43

Swift-Daley detail

Back on Rt 6, 1 mile (1.6km) further, on the left after the Post Office, is a small old house, the **Swift-Daley House and Tool Museum** (open July to August, Monday to Friday 1–4pm), a good example of a full-Cape house and with a tool collection in an old barn in the back.

At the set of lights just beyond is the Town Hall on the right and the **Eastham Windmill** on the left. This is the oldest windmill on Cape Cod, built in Plymouth in the 1680s by Thomas Paine of Eastham, moved to Eastham in 1793, and then here in 1808. Most of the old handhewn machinery is still in place. Continue down Samoset Road, alongside the windmill, to **First Encounter Beach**, where 18 Pilgrims from the *Mayflower* spent the nights of December 6 and 7, 1620. Awoken by raining arrows from the local Nauset Indians on the second morning of their stay, they were discouraged from making the Cape their new home and chose Plymouth instead.

Further along Rt 6 on the right is the **Salt Pond Visitors Center** of the National Seashore (open summer daily 9am–8pm; winter, daily 9am–4.30pm, tel: 255-3421). As well as providing information on the National Seashore trails and the ranger-guided walks, there are displays on local history, industry, architecture and wildlife.

Directly across the street from the visitors center parking lot is the quaint yellow building of the former **one**

Old Coast Guard Station

Nauset Light

room school house (open July to August, Monday to Friday 1:30–4:30pm). Built in 1869 and used as a school until 1936, it now houses Native American artifacts found in the area, farming implements and memorabilia of Henry Beston, author of *The Outermost House* (*see below*).

Take the road out of the parking lot marked to the beaches. This leads to both Coast Guard and Nauset Light Beaches. A right turn at the T-junction at the end of the road leads to **Coast Guard Beach**. Near here was the site of Henry Beston's two-room cottage in which he wrote *The Outermost House* in the late 1920s. The house was washed away to sea during the blizzard of 1978. Another big storm in 1990 revealed the remains of a prehistoric dwelling. Dating back 11,000 years to the Early Archaic era, it was the oldest undisturbed archaeological site in New England. Almost as quickly as it was revealed, this fascinating discovery was covered again by the sea. It remained visible for two summers, just long enough for archaeologists to record what was there.

A left turn at the T-junction will lead to **Nauset Light Beach**, through coastal shrubs and dwarf pines. Nauset lighthouse, painted in a picturesque red and white, stands on private property and can only be viewed from the parking lot. This beach, along with Coast Guard Beach, is popular with summer visitors as well as the many harbor seals who winter here. Take the first right out of the parking lot onto Cable Road. The ★★ **Three Sisters Lighthouses** sit in a grove on the right of the road. There were originally three brick lighthouses at Nauset, placed there in 1838. The brick structures eventually went the way of many buildings on the edge of the sea, and were washed away when the dunes eroded. Three wooden structures were then built on moveable platforms, and came to be known as the Three Sisters.

Follow Cable Road to the T-junction, and turn left to get back to Rt 6.

Nauset Beach

Beaches: in Orleans, **Nauset Beach** (*see page 42*); **Skaket Beach**, on the bay side, off Skaket Beach Road. In Eastham, **Nauset Light** and **Coast Guard Beaches** (*see above*); and bayside beaches **First Encounter Beach** (*see page 43*), and **Campground Landing Beach**, Campground Road off Herring Brook Road.

Ponds: in Orleans, **Crystal Lake**, off Monument Road and **Pilgrim Lake**, off Kescauogansett and Monument Roads; in Eastham, **Herring Pond** and **Great Pond**, off Samoset, Herring Brook and Great Pond Roads.

National Seashore trails: Fort Hill Area (*see page 42*), a short trail with views of Nauset Marsh; from the Visitors Center are two trails, the **Buttonbush Trail** specially designed for the blind, and **Nauset Marsh Trail**.

Wellfleet and Truro

Marconi Station – Wellfleet – Truro – Highland Light
See map, p41

Wellfleet was originally an outpost settlement of Eastham, with prolific oyster beds and large harbors. The town was incorporated in 1763, probably named after Wallfleet in England, famous for its own oyster beds. The landscape and settlements of Wellfleet have changed dramatically over the centuries. Duck Creek, now only a small stream that meanders through salt marshes, used to be a deep water anchorage, and schooners used to tie up where Uncle Tim's Bridge stands today (*see page 47*). There were also four islands off the bay side, three of which (Great, Griffiths and Bound Brook) have since joined the mainland while the fourth (Billingsgate) has been swallowed up by the sea. Traditionally, Wellfleet's economy depended on the sea. By the mid-1800s, half the fish consumed in the United States were caught by Cape Cod fishing boats, and the Wellfleet fleet was second only to Provincetown.

Wellfleet Waymarker

45

The picturesque center of Wellfleet looks much as it did a century ago. Seventy percent of the town is conservation land, which includes protected bayside beaches and long stretches of isolated ocean beaches, kettle ponds, open moorland, and salt marshes.

At the Eastham/Wellfleet border on Rt 6 is the popular **Wellfleet Drive-in** showing outdoor movies in the summer, and indoor movies year round. One of the local treats on a warm summer evening is to fill the car with people, blankets and pillows and head for the drive-in. This is also the location of a large **flea market** (open mid-April to mid-October, Saturday and Sunday 8am–4pm, July and August, also on Wednesday and Thursday).

Flea market merchandise

Continue along Rt 6 almost 2 miles (3.2km) until the National Seashore sign directing the way to the ★ **Marconi Wireless Station Site**. After a lovely drive through National Seashore land, park the car and follow the wooden path to take you to the site of the first US transatlantic wireless telegraph station. The first message transmitted across the ocean was from President Theodore Roosevelt to King Edward VII of England in 1903. The site was dismantled in 1920. The surrounding landscape is typical of the lower Cape's moorland, with meandering paths through scrub pines, wild blueberry and beach plum bushes and tall beach grass. The **Atlantic White Cedar Swamp Trail** leads off from here, a 1.2-mile (2-km) circuit that leads through a cedar swamp. This

Marconi Station

Marking ship time

Historical Society

Looking towards Great Island

is the narrowest part of Cape Cod; from an observation deck you can scan the land from Cape Cod Bay to the Atlantic.

Back on Rt 6, continue towards Provincetown, turning left at the sign for **Wellfleet Center and Harbor**. On your left is **Duck Creek**, the main anchorages of Wellfleet until the arrival of the railroad sealed off the upper half of the Creek to all but small boats, hastening the decline of local commercial fishing. At the fork in the road, continue on Main Street to the center of town. On the right is the imposing white ★★**First Congregational Church**, dating from 1850. The most famous aspect of this church, entitling it to a listing in Ripley's *Believe it or Not*, is its clock, the only town clock in the world that strikes ship time, a complicated system indecipherable to most landlubbers. Inside the church is a rare stained-glass window depicting a 17th-century clipper ship similar to the *Mayflower*, and an old Hook and Hastings organ.

A little further along on the right, is the **Wellfleet Historical Society** (end of June to beginning of September, Tuesday to Friday 10am–noon and 2–5pm; Saturday 2–5pm) housed in a former village shop c1860. The collection focuses on the life and times of Wellfleet.

Main Street now heads into the bustling heart of town. To visit ★ **Wellfleet Harbor**, head down Holbrook Ave and bear right at the intersection with Commercial Street. By the first half of the 20th century, this harbor had so silted up that only a small fishing fleet could anchor here, and even that could enter or leave only at high tide. In the 1950s the channel was dredged and bulkheads constructed, making it one of the best harbors on the Cape.

Wellfleet Harbor is enclosed by the barrier beach formed by the protecting arm of ★ **Great Island**, now attached to the mainland. It is the site of one of the ear-

liest English settlements in the area, and inhabited by Indians for several thousand years before that. The decline in onshore whaling led to the demise of this settlement, and the area is now only inhabited by wildlife. About ¾ mile (1.2km) off Jeremy Point at the tip of Great Island, the island of Billingsgate is now under water. A hundred years ago, there was a thriving fishing community on Billingsgate, with over 30 homes, a school and a lighthouse. As the island was swallowed up by the sea, the houses were floated over to the mainland, a popular practice on other parts of the Cape (*see Provincetown, page50*).

Return to Main Street by taking Commercial Street (bear right at the fork with Holbrook Ave, following the edge of the water). Commercial Street is lined with small restaurants and galleries overlooking the creek and marshes. As the road curves to the right **Uncle Tim's Bridge** comes into view, a 19th-century bridge spanning the salt marshes.

Wellfleet Harbor
Over the salt marshes

Now head towards Truro by turning left onto Rt 6 at the lights ahead.

Truro was the site of several of the Pilgrims' explorations by Myles Standish and his search party, and it was here that they found the Indians' cache of corn that saw them through the first winter in the New World (*see page10*). But it wasn't until the late 1600s that the land was bought from the local Pamet Indians. Originally settled as part of Eastham, the town was dubbed Dangerfield for the treacherous shoals off its coast. Incorporated in 1709, the inhabitants chose the more attractive name of Truro after the Cornish town in England.

Truro's early residents were at the forefront of the whaling industry. Ship-building was also an important industry and the shipyards at Pamet Harbor built brigs and schooners bound for the Grand Banks. Pamet Harbor began to silt up in the mid-1800s, heralding the decline of Truro's fortunes. Today, it is the most remote and sleepy of all the Cape towns, with a year-round population of just 15,000, although in acreage it is one of the largest towns on the Cape. Almost 70 percent of Truro's 42 sq miles (109 sq km) is owned by the National Seashore, and includes some of the most beautiful scenery on the Cape.

As you pass the town line into Truro, and just past Prince Valley Road, there is an old **gas station** once painted by Edward Hopper. Hopper built a house in Truro in the 1930s and summered here until his death in 1967. Continue along Rt 6 then follow signs for Truro Center. Pass through the center (don't blink or you will miss it entirely), and cross the Pamet River. At the fork in the road past the tiny Cobb Library on the right, head to the right and up the hill. At the top of the hill take a steep left turn following signs

Time stands still at
Hopper's gas station

Church with Paul Revere bell

Among the dunes, Corn Hill Beach

48

Highland House

to the Town Hall. Opposite the intersection with Bridge Road is the ★★ **First Congregational Church**, also known as Bell Meetinghouse, on the left down a sandy dirt lane. This lovely white clapboard church was built in 1827 and houses a bell cast by Paul Revere and windows made of Sandwich glass with window catches fashioned into the shape of whales. The church is surrounded by a peaceful old cemetery containing a cenotaph to 57 men who died in a ferocious storm that hit the peninsula in 1841.

Now take a sharp left down the hill on Bridge Road and turn right onto Castle Road. At a fork, take the left-hand road to **Corn Hill Beach**. The hill on the far side of the beach parking lot is where Myles Standish and his search party of 16 men discovered the cache of Indian corn. Taking some of the corn with them, they returned later and took 10 more bushels to plant the following spring.

Corn Hill Beach is a wide bay beach with views across to Provincetown. Walk left for less than 1 mile (under 2km) along the shore to reach the jetty of Pamet Harbor.

Return to Rt 6 by taking a left at Castle Road, and crossing the lovely marshes of the Little Pamet. At Rt 6, turn left towards Provincetown. On the left is the produce stand of **Hillside Farm**, one of only a few working farms on the Outer Cape. Here you will find the best corn on Cape Cod, wonderful fruits and vegetables, plus Portuguese baked goods and local jams and preserves.

Before Rt 6A splits off from Rt 6 towards North Truro Center, the road crosses over a hill, originally known as the Hill of Storms and the site of the first meetinghouse in Truro. The **Old North Cemetery** has graves dating back to 1713. Follow Rt 6A into North Truro. At the intersection with the flashing light (this is North Truro Center), turn left to take you to Pond Village. The Pilgrims' search party spent their second night here on the shore of the pond.

Head back to the flashing light and continue straight, passing under Rt 6 on Highland Road. Turn right at the T-junction and left onto Lighthouse Road, following signs to Cape Cod Light. Today this area seems deserted, but in the 19th century it was scattered with summer hotels and houses. Ahead is one such former hotel, the **Highland House** (open June to September, daily 10am–5pm), which contains the collection of the Truro Historical Society.

Just past the museum is the public **Highland Golf Links** (open April to October). Founded in 1892, it is one of the oldest courses in the country. The setting and views are spectacular, perched as it is on the edge of the dunes overlooking the open Atlantic. From here one can see the white ★★★ **Highland Light** ahead with its black light cage (also called Cape Cod Light), visible 20 miles (32km) out to sea and the brightest on the New England Coast. The original light on this site was erected in 1797,

Highland Light

the first on Cape Cod. It was replaced in 1853, but like many Cape Cod lighthouses eroded into the sea four years later and was replaced. The light was again threatened by erosion recently and has had to be moved back 400ft (120 meters). This should last about 200 hundred years.

South along the dunes from Highland Light is a Gothic-style battlement in the middle of the barren landscape. Called the **Jenny Lind Tower**, it originally formed part of the Fitchburg Railroad Depot in Boston. In 1850 P.T. Barnum, Jenny Lind's promoter, overbooked concert tickets for her tour to Boston. In response, the 'Swedish Nightingale' gave a free concert from this railroad tower. The tower was moved here in 1927 by a Boston attorney when it was slated for demolition.

Back on Rt 6 heading north, at the crest of a hill is a magnificent ★ **view** of Provincetown ahead and on the right the dunes and marshes surrounding **Pilgrim Lake**, once Truro's East Harbor.

Beaches: In Wellfleet, **Marconi Beach**, a National Seashore beach, follow signs from Rt 6, and **White Crest Beach** and **Cahoon Hollow Beach**, town beaches, both accessible from Ocean View Drive off Cahoon Hollow Road; on the bay side, **Mayo Beach**, on Kendrick Ave. In Truro, **Head of the Meadow Beach** on the ocean side, off Rt 6, and **Corn Hill Beach** on the bay side off Corn Hill Road (*see page 48*).

49

Conservation areas: The **Wellfleet Bay Wildlife Sanctuary** covers 800 acres (323 hectares) of salt marsh, pine woods, fields, pond and moorland and has 5 miles (8km) of trails. The 8-mile/13-km **Great Island Trail**, Chequesset Neck Road, is the most difficult of the National Seashore trails, but well worth it. In Truro there are nature walks from the **Pilgrim Heights**, off Rt 6, plus a lovely stretch of ocean beach

Truro's sands

Tour 8

Provincetown

Commercial Street – Provincetown Art Association and Museum – Macmillan Wharf – Pirate Ship *Whydah* – Pilgrim Monument – Universalist Church

Provincetown Harbor

The sandy closed fist at the end of the flexed arm of Cape Cod, **Provincetown** evokes the quintessential New England fishing village. It embodies many qualities of the rest of the Cape yet is also very different. It has always shown a mind of its own, with a long history as a haven for visual artists, writers and a large gay community.

The Pilgrims' first footsteps in the New World were on the shores of Provincetown. The *Mayflower Compact*, the first document of self governance in the New World and the precursor to the US Constitution, was written while the ship was anchored in this harbor and the *Mayflower*'s passengers spent five weeks here looking for a suitable place to settle before deciding to head to Plymouth. Originally part of Truro, Provincetown was incorporated in 1727 and went on to become a major whaling port, second only to Nantucket and New Bedford.

Festive in Provincetown

50

In 1818 a settlement was started on Long Point, the long sand bar that encloses Provincetown Harbor, on account of the large shoals of fish nearby. When the fish moved elsewhere, the homes were floated across the harbor and repositioned, mostly in the west end of town. These houses can be identified by their blue enamel plaques.

The most interesting aspect of the Provincetown land-

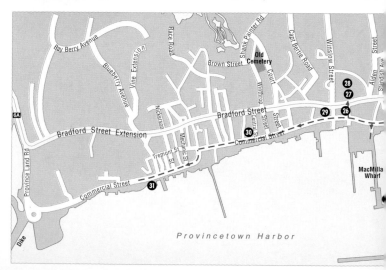

scape is its large expanse of parabolic sand dunes in the Province Lands, an area stretching from Rt 6 to the ocean. Sand is the essential element of this part of the Cape and human habitation is in constant battle against it. Many artists and writers have sought inspiration in these dunes, living in shacks made of driftwood. Some of them still stand today (*see page 60*).

At Province Lands

In the height of summer, a car becomes a hindrance in Provincetown, so park in one of the municipal or private lots and strike out on foot. This tour starts from the east end of Commercial Street and heads west. An informative way to see the principal sites is by taking the **Provincetown Trolley** which runs along Commercial Street and continues on to the National Seashore. The trolley can be picked up outside the Town Hall every half hour from 10am to 4pm and hourly until 8pm in the summer.

The east end of Commercial Street retains the feeling of a quiet fishing town, with its pretty gardens and little lanes, and views of the harbor between every house. This is also the birthplace of the famous Provincetown Players. Past Conway Street, on the left, is a plaque marking the former site of Lewis Wharf **16**, where the Provincetown Players performed their first plays in 1915–16, an event which changed the course of American theater (*see pages 61–2*). The white house next to this site, number 571, is the former home of the writer **John Dos Passos**.

No 524 Commercial Street was the birthplace of the famous Arctic explorer Donald B. MacMillan **17**, who also later lived at No 473. Look in the Provincetown Museum for exhibits about his life (*see page 52*). At the corner of

Beached in Provincetown

John Dos Passos' house

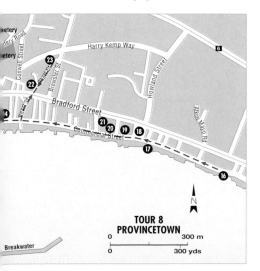

TOUR 8
PROVINCETOWN

0 — 300 m
0 — 300 yds

Commercial and Howland stands the large former **Eastern Schoolhouse** ⑱, one of three schools built in 1844. It now houses two galleries, the Long Point Gallery, where some of Provincetown's best-known contemporary artists such as Robert Motherwell, are shown, and downstairs, the co-operative Rising Tide Gallery.

Number 476, the **Figurehead House** ⑲, is named for the lovely figurehead found floating in the Indian Ocean by a Captain Henry Cook in 1867. It is said to have originally been the full figure of a woman, and that the captain had the bottom half of her sawn off while still at sea. Only her top half graces the house today. No 466 Commercial Street is an old shingled Cape house known as the **Kibbe Cook House** ⑳, the former home of Mary Heaton Vorse, one of the first writers to live in Provincetown. She wrote a wonderful book on life in Provincetown in the first half of the 20th century called *Time and the Town*.

Provincetown Art Association

Just past the Cook house on the corner of Bangs Street stands the ★★★ **Provincetown Art Association and Museum** ㉑ (open winter, Saturday and Sunday noon–5pm; spring and fall, daily noon–5pm and Friday and Saturday 8–10pm; summer, daily noon–5pm and 8–10pm). Organized in 1914 by a group of artists, including Charles Hawthorne, the association is one of the foremost art museums in the country, with Milton Avery and Marsden Hartley among its members.

Past the Art Association, Commercial Street fills up with stores and restaurants. Turn right onto Pearl Street, cross Bradford Street which runs parallel to Commercial, and on your left you will come to the **Fine Arts Work Center** ㉒ (24 Pearl Street), which offers 10 artists and 10 writers resident placements each winter. As well as a gallery, there are readings, seminars and workshops held throughout the year. Continuing along Pearl Street, at the bend in the road stand the studios ㉓ of two of the town's most influential artists, **Edwin W. Dickinson**, who worked and lived at No 46 Pearl Street, and **Charles Hawthorne**, whose studio was at No 48.

Heritage Museum
A night out in Provincetown

Back on Commercial Street, at the corner with Center, is the imposing white former Methodist Church built in 1860. From 1958–74, it was run by Walter Chrysler (of automobile fame) as a fine-art museum. It is now home to the **Provincetown Heritage Museum** ㉔ (open Memorial Day to Columbus Day, daily 10am–6pm), with art works, nautical artifacts, and a half-scale model of the *Rose Dorothea*, the largest indoor boat model in the world.

From this point Commercial is packed with shops, galleries and cafes. A little further, on the left, is ★★ **MacMillan Wharf** ㉕, named after the Arctic explorer (in the town's fishing heyday, most houses along Provincetown harbor had their own wharf). MacMillan Wharf still plays

an important role in the fishing industry; in the afternoon the day's catch is unloaded from the town's fishing fleet here. This is also the location of the fascinating ★★ **Pirate Ship *Whydah* Museum** (open summer, daily 9am–7pm, winter, tel: 487-3488). In 1982, Barry Clifford, a native of Brewster, uncovered the *Whydah*, wrecked of the coast off Wellfleet in 1717, the first pirate ship to be discovered in these waters. Some of the restoration is taking place on view at the museum on MacMillan Wharf, and exhibits include cannons, gold pieces, shoes, and a large iron bell inscribed with the name *Whydah*.

Back on Commercial Street is the imposing ★ **Town Hall** 26 on the corner of Ryder. Built in 1880, the build ing still houses the town offices, as well as a collection of paintings donated by some of Provincetown's famous artists. The upstairs auditorium hosts concerts in the sum mer (tel: 487-7000 for information).

In a small park behind Town Hall, where Ryder inter sects with Bradford, is a bas relief 27 commemorating the signing of the *Mayflower Compact*. On the hill behind is Provincetown's most famous building, the ★★ **Pilgrim Monument** 28 (built in 1907–10), copied from the Torre del Mangia in Siena. It may seem an incongruous choice of design for a small New England fishing village, but it is hard to imagine Provincetown without its turrets tow ering overhead. The ★★★ **view** from the top of the tower is worth the uphill trudge; on a clear day, one can see 30 miles (48km) to Boston. At the base of the tower is the **Provincetown Museum** containing memorabilia of Don ald MacMillan, old photographs, artifacts from the Provincetown Players and the town's oldest fire engine built to navigate the thick sand of Provincetown's byways.

Head back to Commercial Street down Ryder, turning right at the Town Hall to continue to the west end. Past Gosnold and set back from the street is the handsome

*Commercial Street
MacMillan Wharf*

Pilgrim Monument

Universalist Church

★★ **Universalist Church 29**, built in 1847 but with origins further back than that. In 1820, *Mayflower* descendants Sylvia and Elizabeth Freeman found on the beach a waterlogged book, *The Life of Rev John Murray – Preacher of Universal Salvation*, which became instrumental in the founding of this church. Inside are some interesting *trompe l'oeil* murals by Carl Wendt. Look, too, for the medallions on the pews which are carved of whale teeth and the chandelier which is made of Sandwich glass.

Commercial Street continues westward. Past Central Street at No 160 is an impressive Georgian-colonial style residence, the **Grozier House 30**, built in 1830 by Captain John Atkins. The tower at the top of the three-story building was used by his wife to watch for his return; from this point she had a 360 degree view of Provincetown Harbor, Boston Harbor, and the open ocean.

At No 59 is the **Center for Coastal Studies 31** (tel: 487-3622), dedicated to research and public education for marine and coastal environments. The CCS has played a major role in increasing public awareness of the plight of the whale population and in the process has spawned a growing interest in whale watching. There is an ongoing program of lectures and presentations at the center.

Commercial Street ends at the rotary ahead, where the Pilgrims are thought to have first stepped foot in the New World. Also here is a wonderful view towards the harbor and the center of town on the left, the tidal marshes to the right, and the broad stone ★ **breakwater** that stretches one mile across the harbor to Longpoint.

There are several other places well worth visiting by car. Set in the midst of the ★★ **Province Lands Dunes**, the National Seashore's **Province Lands Visitors Center** (open mid-April to early December, daily 9am–5pm) offers exhibits and films about the natural and maritime history of the area, and information on trails, vehicle hire and beaches. Past the Visitors Center is the ★ **Old Life Saving Station** (open July to August, daily 10am–4pm), in an old US Life Saving Station towed here by barge from Chatham. It tells the story of the 'surfmen' who patrolled the outer beaches of the Cape on the look-out for ships in distress; demonstrations of rescue methods are held on Thursday in July and August, at 6.30pm. Also here is **Race Point Beach**, from where Thoreau wrote 'Here a man can stand and put all America behind him.'

Old Life Saving Station
A bird's-eye view

Beaches and conservation areas: Beech Forest, on Race Point Road, with pond, forests and trails, plus a bicycle trail through the dunes to **Herring Cove Beach** (to drive to Herring Cove Beach, which is more sheltered than Race Point, follow Province Lands Road, off Race Point Road).

54

Excursion to Plymouth

Plimoth Plantation – Burial Hill – Plymouth Rock –
Mayflower II – Mayflower Society Museum – Pilgrim
Hall Museum – Cranberry World

Plymouth, where the Pilgrims built their little settlement
in the wilds of the New World in the winter of 1620, makes
a good excursion from Cape Cod, for the history of the
Cape is tied to this town. The principal sights center on the
early Pilgrim history, some of them fascinating, some more
commercial. Also here are several stunning examples of
18th- and 19th-century architecture.

The best place to start your exploration is at the well-
loved ★★★ **Plimoth Plantation** ❷ (open April to November, daily 9am–5pm). This living history museum
offers a fascinating glimpse into life in the early days of

At Plimoth Plantation

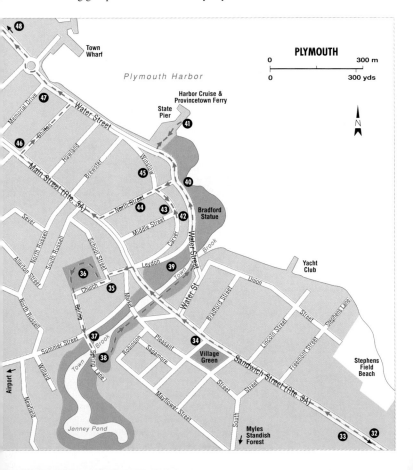

Plimoth Plantation and
Hobbamock's Homesite

the colony. As one walks along the dusty street, wandering into tiny one-room cabins made of hand-hewn wood, actor pilgrims go about their daily chores. They speak in the accent of the period on any subject you care to discuss, as long as it is relevant to a time prior to 1627. Nearby is the recreated Wampanoag camp, **Hobbamock's Homesite**, where Native Americans, dressed in traditional clothes, go about their own chores; they, however, discuss their heritage from a 20th-century perspective.

As you head along Rt 3A towards the center of Plymouth, there are two houses worth a look. The **Harlow Old Fort House** ③③ (119 Sandwich Street/Rt 3A, varied opening times, tel: 746-0012) was built in 1677 and is devoted to life in the late 17th century. About ¼ mile (0.4 km) further into town is **Howland House** ③④ (33 Sandwich Street, open Memorial Day to Columbus Day and Thanksgiving weekend, tours daily at 10am and 4:30pm), the only building still standing in which original *Mayflower* passengers once lived.

Continue into the center of town, park your car and start your walking tour at **Town Square**. Here you will find the **1749 Courthouse** ③⑤, the oldest wooden courthouse still standing in America. Follow the red brick steps that lead to the top of ★ **Burial Hill** ③⑥ (good views out to the harbor and the *Mayflower II*) where a number of original *Mayflower* passengers are buried. Take the path leading down the side of the hill to Summer Street. Ahead on the other side of the street is the **Sparrow House** ③⑦ (open daily except Wednesday, 10am–5pm), built in 1640 and the oldest house in Plymouth. As well as rooms with period furnishings, there is a pottery studio where glazed stoneware is made using traditional methods.

Turn left down Spring Lane just past the Sparrow House. Here is the pretty Jenney Pond on the right and the reconstructed **Jenney Grist Mill** ③⑧ on the left. Follow

Burial Hill

the path along the brook through **Brewster Gardens** **❸** to the harbor.

Plymouth's original settlement was sited on the hill to the west side of the brook. Make your way to Water Street; ahead is the famous ★ **Plymouth Rock** **❹**, claimed to be the stone the Pilgrims first stepped on when they came ashore in Plymouth. Nearby is the ★ *Mayflower II* **❹** (same opening times as Plimoth Plantation), a reconstruction built in England and sailed to Plymouth in 1957. Across Water Street from the rock is **Coles Hill** **❹**, the Pilgrims' first burial ground. During their first winter, nearly half the settlers died; most of them were buried under the cover of night to hide the truth of their dwindling numbers from the Indians. On this same hill is a larger than life **statue of Massasoit**, the great sachem with whom the Pilgrims signed treaties in that first year. Here also is the **Plymouth National Wax Museum** **❹** (open March to June and October to November, daily 9am–5pm, July to September, daily 9am–9pm) where the history of the Pilgrims is brought to life in wax .

Plymouth Rock and the 'Mayflower II'

Turn left on Carver Street, in front of the museum and left again onto North Street. The **Spooner House** **❹** (27 North Street, same hours as the Harlow Old Fort House, *see previous page*), built in 1747, displays exhibits about the changing tastes and occupations in Plymouth from pre-Revolutionary days to the 1950s. Return towards the harbor and turn left onto Winslow Street for the ★★ **Mayflower Society Museum** **❹** (open July to mid-September, daily 10am–4pm, rest of the year, tel: 746-2590). This magnificent 1754 home reflects the pre-Revolutionary era and the late 19th century when affluent visitors flocked to New England coastal towns.

57

The ★★ **Pilgrim Hall Museum** **❹** (open February to December, daily 9:30am–4:30pm), three blocks down Main Street on the corner of Chilton Street, is the oldest public museum in the country. Inside are a wide array of Pilgrim artifacts and displays about the Wampanoag, plus the recovered remains of the *Sparrowhawk*, c1626, the first recorded shipwreck off Cape Cod.

Walk down Chilton to Water Street and turn left to get to the **Hedge House Museum** **❹** (open same hours as the Harlow Old Fort House, *see previous page*). This handsome yellow Federal-style house was built in 1809 as the home of a merchant ship owner. Inside is an interesting exhibit on textiles featuring historic clothing, samplers and quilts. Continue down Water Street, past the Tourist Information Center and Town Wharf to **Cranberry World** **❹** (225 Water Street, open May to November, daily 9.30am–5pm). Attractions include small cranberry bogs, cooking demonstrations (plus free cranberry refreshments) and antique and modern tools of the trade.

At Cranberry World

Cultural History

The visual arts

The great whaling days of the 19th century sent Cape Cod men traveling around the world in search of their prey. These sailors brought home not only foreign goods and trinkets but a broadened perspective which helped create, in this rural area, a cosmopolitan atmosphere rare for the time. As the historian Henry Kittredge put it, 'Narrow-mindedness found barren soil in a district where two houses out of three belonged to men who knew half the seaports of the world and had lived ashore for months at a time in foreign countries.'

Exposure to new ideas was perhaps one of the factors which helped produce on Cape Cod one of America's most important art colonies. By the end of the 19th century, art colonies were sprouting up in Europe in reaction to the conventional academic training of the time.

Charles Hawthorne, enchanted by the beauty and remoteness of Provincetown, opened his Cape Cod School of Art in 1899. His aim was to get students to work directly from nature, using the setting of Provincetown as their subject matter – a radical idea at the time. The school was an immediate success, attracting such new talents as Edwin Dickinson, Ross Moffett and Henry Henche. By 1916, there were five more art schools in town.

The years 1910–20 were an exciting time in Provincetown. There came a steady stream of artists, writers, actors and playwrights, many of whom went on to become major American talents. The Provincetown Art Association was founded in 1914 by a group of five artists, including Hawthorne, who donated a painting each. The premise was 'to promote education of the public in the arts, and social intercourse between artists and laymen.' The Association had its first exhibition the following year and went on to become one of the foremost small museums in the country with a notable collection of work by the many artists who have passed through town.

By the early 1920s a new group of artists and writers of a more modern bent had formed, revelling in a new-found sense of sexual and political freedom. Among these were artists Marsden Hartley and Charles Demuth, and John Reed, author of *Ten Days that Shook the World*, the famous account of the Soviet Revolution.

The old school artists, headed by Hawthorne, opposed the rapid changes affecting the modern world, embodied in the art and ideals of the new arrivals. Tensions between the old and new school mounted and the conservatives barred the modernists from the Provincetown Art Association until a compromise was agreed whereby the two groups had separate exhibition space, an

Opposite page:
Edward Hopper's
'The Long Leg'

Hawthorne's 'The First Voyage'

59

Edwin Dickinson

Hawthorne painting class, c1920

Hopper's 'Gas'

arrangement which continued until 1937. The traditionalists included Richard Miller and Frederick Waugh, and the modernists were headed by Ross Moffett, E. Ambrose Webster, Karl Knaths and Max Bohm.

Shacks built of driftwood and set in the Provinceland Dunes were popular among early artists and writers, and have continued to be over the years. Such famous creative minds as Jack Kerouac, Tennessee Williams, e. e. cummings, Norman Mailer and Jackson Pollock have all spent time working in these isolated dwellings. The painter Loren MacIver and her poet husband, Floyd Frankenberg, lived in a shack year-round from the 1920s to the 1940s.

In 1930, Edward Hopper began spending summers in Truro and continued to do so every year until his death in the 1960s. His images of the Outer Cape are world famous. Surrealism came to Provincetown in the mid 1930s with the arrival of Arshile Gorky, Roberto Matta and Max Ernst. Hans Hofmann, an abstract expressionist who had fled from Hitler's Germany, opened the School of Modern Art in 1935. Hofmann's school operated in Provincetown in summer and New York in winter and soon became the focal point of the local arts movement, drawing Lee Krasner, Jackson Pollock, Larry Rivers and Fritz Bultman.

During the next 20 years, Provincetown became a focus of the national art world, in particular the abstract expressionist movement, attracting such luminaries as Helen Frankenthaler, Robert Motherwell, Franz Kline, Mark Rothko and Milton Avery. The 1950s brought to town an avant-garde group of artists, including Alex Katz, Red Grooms and Robert Beauchamp, the performances of their 'happenings' often outraging the locals.

The foundation of the Fine Arts Work Center in 1968 aimed to bring new talent to Provincetown and provide work and living space for emerging artists and writers.

This organization enables 10 artists and 10 writers each year to work and live in this inspiring environment.

Provincetown continues to foster a vibrant arts scene, although on a more commercial footing than in the days of Charles Hawthorne. Artists still flock here from around the world and both the successful and the relatively unknown are exhibited in the many galleries in town.

Here is a listing of the most highly respected galleries in town: **DNA Gallery**, 288 Bradford Street, tel: 6287-7700; **Berta Walker Gallery**, two locations: 208 Bradford Street, tel: 487-6411 and 153 Commercial Street, tel: 487-8794 (called **Walker's Wonders**); **Julie Heller Gallery**, 2 Gosnold Street, tel: 487-2169; **Long Point Gallery**, 492 Commercial Street, tel: 487-1795; **Rising Tide Gallery**, 494 Commercial Street, tel: 487-4037; **UFO Gallery**, 424 Commercial Street, tel: 487-4424; and in Wellfleet, the **Cherry Stone Gallery**, 70 East Commercial Street, tel: 349-3026.

Berta Walker Gallery

61

Writers

Although not belonging to a unified school like the visual artists, writers of all kinds have been drawn to Cape Cod. Many use their surroundings as topics for their writing, while others simply enjoy working in such a beautiful and inspiring setting.

One of the earliest of the former group was Henry David Thoreau who wrote *Cape Cod,* an acount of three long walks along the Atlantic beach from Nauset to Provincetown in the mid-1800s. In this book he records his observations of both the natural world and the solitary lives of many of the people he encountered, from lighthouse keepers and oystermen to shipwreck scavengers.

Henry Beston's book, *The Outermost House*, recounts a year spent on the remote Nauset Beach from 1927–28, a powerful chronicle of the sights, sounds and seasons around him. Explaining his reasons for writing the book, he said: 'The world today is sick to its thin blood for the lack of elemental things, for fire before the hands, for water welling from the earth, for air, for the dear earth itself underfoot.'

The writers who have visited and been inspired by Cape Cod are too numerous to list, but among those who have lived here are Conrad Aiken, Tennessee Williams, John Dos Passos, Norman Mailer, Stanley Kunitz, Mary Oliver, Marge Piercy and Annie Dillard.

Thoreau

Theater

In the region of Washington Square or Greenwich Village, or...among the sand dunes of Cape Cod – we must look for the real birthplace of the American Drama.' So wrote William Archer about the now legendary Province-

Academy Playhouse

town Players. In 1915, a radical group of writers, playwrights and amateur actors set up a small cooperative-style theater on a disused fish wharf in the east end of Provincetown. Those involved included Mary Heaton Vorse, Susan Glaspell, George Cram Cook and the as yet undiscovered Eugene O'Neill. It was here that the first stage production of O'Neill's *Bound East for Cardiff* was performed. After two summer seasons the theater moved to New York, and went on to become one of the most influential forces in modern American theater. In eight seasons they produced 97 plays by 57 American playwrights.

In 1923, a group calling themselves the Wharf Players tried to take up where the Provincetown Players left off, but conflict within the group quickly spawned the Barnstormers. The producer of the Barnstormers, Raymond Moore, moved to Dennis in 1927 to found the Cape Playhouse, where he aimed 'to stand for the best in the field of art and to establish something infinitely more important than a commercial theater.' The list of actors in his productions reads like a Who's Who of the celebrity world, from Basil Rathbone to Bette Davis, Gregory Peck, Henry Fonda and Humphrey Bogart. The Cape Playhouse continues to run a summer season each year.

Today nearly every town supports a local theater. The most well known are: the **Barnstable Comedy Club**, the oldest amateur theater in the country; the **Highfield Theater** in Falmouth, where the College Light Opera Company puts on musicals; the **Cape Playhouse** in Dennis, (*see above*); the **Monomoy Theatre** in Chatham, home of the Ohio University Players who perform dramas and musicals; **The Cape Cod Reperatory Theatre** in Brewster which presents Shakespeare in an open-air amphitheater; **The Academy Playhouse** in Orleans whose productions range from Shakespeare to musicals; and the **Wellfleet Harbor Actors' Theater**, for avant-garde productions.

Wellfleet Harbor Actors' Theater

Festivals

The following is a list of some of the local festivities held throughout the year. Call the Town Chambers of Commerce (*see page 75*) for dates and further information.

May **Great Race Weekend**, the largest sailboat race in New England sets off from Hyannis and ends in Nantucket.

June **Hyannis Harbor Festival**, blessing of the fleet in Bismore Park. **Heritage Cape Cod**, Cape-wide event held at a variety of venues, including local museums, historical societies and the National Seashore. **Blessing of the Fleet** at MacMillan Wharf in Provincetown, celebration with boats decked out in flags.

July **Fourth of July**, events throughout the Cape, including boat parade and fireworks in Hyannis, parade and fireworks in Provincetown, blessing of the fleet and fireworks in Falmouth. **Mashpee Wampanoag Pow Wow**, Native American celebration by the Wampanoag Tribal Council. **Barnstable County Fair**, in East Falmouth with music, livestock, horticulture, cooking and craft exhibits.

63

August **Cape Cod Air Show**, two-day event at the Otis Air Force Base in Bourne. **Falmouth Road Race**, world class 7.1-mile (11.4-km) race (register by the end of March). **Sails around Cape Cod**, 140-mile (225-km) race beginning and ending in Harwichport. **Chatham Festival of the Arts** in Chase Park. **Carnival Week**, in Provincetown, ending with a Mardi-Gras style parade.

October **Seaside Festival**, in Yarmouth with jugglers, fireworks, games, races and parade. **Women's Week**, in Provincetown, featuring women artists and entertainers. **Fantasia Fair**, in Provincetown, 10-day event for transvestites.

At the Fantasia Fair
Preparing for Thanksgiving

November **Old Fashioned Thanksgiving Celebration**, craft demonstrations, exhibits and holiday food at the Green Briar Nature Center, Sandwich. **Thanksgiving festivities** also held at Plimoth Plantation.

December **Christmas** celebrations throughout the Cape.

Food and Drink

Opposite: a leisurely place to shop

Surrounded as it is by sea, the Cape's most abundant food is fish, always freshly caught and delicious. Along with its famous cod are blue fish, stripped bass, halibut, flounder, haddock and pollock.

Shellfish is also widely available, and the crowning glory on Cape menus is a platter of freshly shucked Wellfleet oysters. Some say there are no better oysters in the world. Clams come in a variety of sizes and guises. Quahogs (pronounced cohogs) are a local hardshell variety, called cherrystones when they are small and littlenecks when they are medium sized. They are best eaten raw. When they are large and a bit tougher, they tend to end up in chowders, pies or in clam sauces served over pasta. Clams can also be served up fried, a delicious treat.

Steamers, the soft shelled variety of clam, also called longnecks, are usually served steamed in a broth of butter and water and eaten with one's fingers. Giant sea clams, 5–6 inches (12–15cm) across, are too tough to be eaten on their own but make a delicious chowder. If you have the chance to attend a clam bake on the beach, where clams are slowly cooked in a sand pit filled with burning embers, take it: it's an experience you will not quickly forget. Mussels are usually steamed simply in water, with a bit of wine and lemon to preserve their delicate flavor. Scallops, on the other hand, are cooked in a variety of ways, from deep fried to delicately steamed.

For some, a visit to Cape Cod would be incomplete without a full lobster dinner – bib, melted butter and all. Lobster used to be so plentiful here that it was only eaten out of necessity and tended to be fed to prisoners and indentured servants up to three times a day. Today it is a pricey, if delicious, meal with the cost dependent on market price. Some of the best places to indulge in a lobster feast are the small and informal lobster or clam shacks found throughout the Cape. Another delicious way to eat lobster is in a lobster roll – a light lobster salad served in a hot dog bun.

There are a number of native fruits to be found on Cape Cod. Cultivated cranberry bogs are visible throughout the Upper and Mid Cape and there are still some wild bogs, mostly within the National Seashore. Beach plums can be found growing near the seashore and although tart when eaten raw, they are made into delicious jams and jellies. Rosehips, the fruit of the fragrant beach roses, are also made into a tasty jelly high in vitamin C. The small wild blueberries seen growing throughout the Cape have a sweetness and flavor far superior to the plump but often bland cultivated ones. In season they can be bought at local farm stands.

Cape Cod is famed for its fish

65

Hard to resist
Dining out

Take your pick

Restaurants

The range of restaurants on Cape Cod is enormous, varying from humble clam shacks to haute cuisine establishments. Some of the best and freshest food can be had in the most simple surroundings but one can also find truly innovative cooking in the more expensive eateries. Some restaurants stay open year round, often with limited weekend opening times in winter, while others open only for the summer. To avoid disappointment, call ahead. Reservations are required at the more popular restaurants in high season. **$** = $10 or under, **$$** = $10-20, **$$$** = over $20

Sandwich

$ Marshlands, 109 Rt 6A at Tupper Rd, tel: 888-9824. Good home cooking in an informal friendly setting.
$ The Dunbar Tea Shop, 1 Water Street, tel: 833-2485. Traditional tea served with fresh scones. Also serves light breakfasts and lunches.
$$ Dan'l Webster Inn, 149 Main Street, tel: 888-3623, (800) 444-3566. Set in a reconstructed colonial tavern. The food is very fresh and tasty.

Bourne

$$ The Chart Room, Shipyard Lane, Cataumet, tel: 563-5350. Dine on fresh seafood while watching the sunset over the marina.

Seasonal refreshment

Falmouth Area

$$$ The Regatta of Falmouth, 217 Clinton Ave, Falmouth, tel: 548-5400. One of the best restaurants on the Cape. Continental and ethnic cuisines. There is also a branch in Cotuit, tel: 428-5715.
$$ Domingo's Olde Restaurant, 856 Rt 28A, W. Falmouth, tel: 540-0575. Delicious Mediterranean-style food served in an 1840s Greek Revival house.

$ The Clam Shack, 227 Clinton Ave, Falmouth, tel: 540-7758. Repeatedly voted best clam shack by *Cape Cod Life*. The clams and the views are great.

Mashpee

$$ The Flume, Lake Ave off Rt 130, tel: 477-1456. Earl Mills, member of the Wampanoag tribe, is the owner and chef of this justly popular restaurant. Traditional favorites are served with creative flair.

Barnstable Area

$$$ Alberto's Ristorante, 360 Main Street, Hyannis, tel: 778-1770. Delicious food with a Northern Italian bent.
$$$ East Bay Lodge, 199 East Bay Road, Osterville, tel: 428-5200. Excellent continental cuisine with over 450 wines, and lavish Sunday brunch.
$ Craigville Pizza and Mexican, 618 Craigville Beach Road, W. Hyannisport, tel: 775-2267, and 4 Barlows Landing Road, Pocasset, tel: 564-6306. Popular with locals.

Yarmouth

$$ Inaho, 157 Main Street, Yarmouthport, tel: 362-5522. Japanese cuisine featuring excellent sushi and sashimi.
$ Jack's Outback, 161 Main Street, Yarmouthport, tel: 362-6690. This is a local institution which specializes in down home cooking.

67

Dennis

$$$ The Red Pheasant Inn, 905 Main Street, Dennis, tel: 385-2133. In the romantic setting of an 18th-century ship's chandlery. Excellent food.
$ Marshside, 25 Bridge Street, E. Dennis, tel: 385-4010. Family oriented favorite open year round.
$ The Ice Cream Smuggler, 716 Main Street, Dennis, tel: 385-5307. Come here for some of the best home-made ice cream around.

Two of many options

Brewster

$$$ Chillingworth Restaurant, 2449 Main Street, Brewster, tel: 896-3640. Its seven-course *prix-fixe* French dinner is one of the best dining experiences on the Cape.
$ Cobie's, 3260 Main Street, E. Brewster, tel: 896-7021. Classic clam shack in business since the 1940s.

Harwich

$$$ Thompson's Clam Bar, 600 Main Street, Harwichport, tel: 430-1239. Hearty fare featuring seafood and old fashioned desserts.
$ Bonnatt's Bakery, 537 Rt 28, Harwichport, tel: 432-7199. A good place to come for breakfast or to buy your picnic lunch.

Chatham

$$$ Chatham Bars Inn, Shore Road, Chatham, tel: 945-0096/(800)527-4884. The excellent food more than matches the stunning views overlooking the sea.

$ Blue Moon Deli-Bistro, 1715 Main Street, W. Chatham. Great breakfasts and snacks at good prices.

$ Marion's Pie Shop, 2022 Main Street, W. Chatham, tel: 432-9439. Home-made pies from lemon meringue to clam or chicken, with great cinnamon rolls and fruit breads.

Orleans

Nauset Beach Club

$$$ Nauset Beach Club, 222 East Main Street, E. Orleans, tel: 255-8547. Northern Italian cuisine with a Cape Cod edge. Very popular so get here early as no reservations are taken.

$$ Capt Cass Rock Harbor Seafood, 117 Rock Harbor Road, Orleans, no phone. Authentic clam shack serving very fresh seafood since the 1950s.

Eastham

$$ Eastham Lobster Pool, 4380 Rt 6, N. Eastham, tel: 255-9706/255-3314 for take-out. Basic surroundings serving fresh fish cooked many different ways.

Wellfleet

$$$ Aesop's Tables, 316 Main Street, Wellfleet, tel: 349-6450. Festive but not too formal, serving deliciously fresh fish and produce from the restaurant's own farm.

$$ Flying Fish Cafe, Briar Lane, Wellfleet, tel: 349-3100. Innovative tasty food in an informal setting, home-made breads and pastries.

Bayside Lobster Hutt

$$ Bayside Lobster Hutt, Commercial Street, Box 703, Wellfleet, tel: 349-6333. The freshest no-frills seafood around, served in a 19th-century oyster shanty.

Truro

$$ Adrian's, Rt 6 between Head of the Meadow and High Head, N. Truro, tel: 487-4360. Adventurous breakfasts, delicious pizzas and other Italian specialties.

Provincetown

$$$ Front Street, 230 Commercial Street, tel: 487-9715. One of the first places in town to offer haute cuisine.

$$$ Ciro and Sal's, 4 Kiley Court, Provincetown, tel: 487-0049. Subterranean Italian trattoria. Rich hearty food.

$$$ Napi's, 7 Freeman Street, Provincetown, tel: 487-1145. A year-round favorite serving a variety of cuisines, including vegetarian, Italian, Chinese and seafood.

$ Spiritus Pizza, 190 Commercial Street, Provincetown, tel: 487-2808. The place to be at 1am when it becomes the happening scene. Also in Hyannis, tel: 775-2955.

Spiritus night action

Shopping

One of the biggest draws for visitors is the chance to go 'antiquing' along the Old King's Highway, Rt 6A. There are innumerable antique stores bordering this ancient route from Sandwich to Orleans, most of them housed in old Cape Cod homes. Although it is rather unlikely that you will find a 17th-century treasure at a thrift store price, much of the pleasure is in the looking, and the range of choice is enormous. There are also a number of auction houses where you may find some genuinely good buys.

For a directory of antique dealers in the area contact the **Cape Cod Antique Dealers Association**, tel: 420-0220. **Destinations**, tel: (800)333-4667, has a more selective listing. The monthly publication *Antiques and Arts* is another source worth checking out. The **Flea Market** at the Wellfleet Drive-In (*see page 45*) is also a good place to browse.

Happy hunting
At the flea market

Bookstores, crafts shops and galleries also proliferate on the Cape. Excellent antiquarian, used and well-stocked bookstores reflect the fact that a large number of writers and intellectuals spend time here. A few special ones to search out are **Parnassus Books**, Rt 6A, Yarmouthport, tel: 362-6420, **Herridge Books**, 11 Main Street, Wellfleet, tel: 349-1323, **West Main Books**, West Main Street, Wellfleet, tel: 349-2095, **Yellow Umbrella Books**, 501 Main Street, Chatham, tel: 945-0144.

Local crafts range in quality, some stores catering more to the tourist trade than to a high quality market. But some produce truly individual and creative products. Three organizations with listings are: **Society of Cape Cod Craftsmen**, Box 1709, Wellfleet 02667; **Artisans' Guild of Cape Cod**, tel: 394-4366; **Cape Cod Potters**, Box 76, Chatham 02633.

For galleries, the main centers are Provincetown and Wellfleet (for a listing see *Culture, page 61*). Look out for the *Provincetown Gallery Guide*, produced by the Provincetown Gallery Guild, Box 242, Provincetown 02657, and *Provincetown Arts*, a glossy annual magazine which is the bible of the local arts scene.

The main shopping districts are in Chatham, Hyannis, Wellfleet and Provincetown, with smaller centers in Falmouth and Osterville. Hyannis has the largest Main Street, lined with many stores, plus the Cape's only real Mall, on Rts 132 and 28. Chatham's shops tend to cater to a more upmarket and conservative clientele. Wellfleet and Provincetown offer an array of sophisticated, unusual and even outrageous shops. Also worth mentioning are the **Christmas Tree Shops**, with locations throughout the Upper and Mid Cape. They sell everything from thumb tacks to furniture.

Provincetown store

The Cape Cod Rail Trail
Along Cape Cod Canal

Active Vacations

Cape Cod is the ideal destination for those looking for a vacation packed with outdoor fun.

Cycling

Not only are the many back roads tempting to cyclists but the Cape is also criss-crossed with bike trails through some of the loveliest scenery in the area. The **Cape Cod Rail Trail** follows the old right of way of the Pennsylvania Central Railroad from Dennis to South Wellfleet, a beautiful and flat trail that is over 20 miles (32km) long. The **Cape Cod Canal** is lined on both sides by bike trails, each 8 miles (13km) in length. The **Falmouth Shining Sea Trail** also follows a disused railroad bed through woodland and along Nantucket Sound from Falmouth Center to Woods Hole. Within the National Seashore are several bike paths, the loveliest being those in the **Province Lands** in Provincetown, leading through undulating sand dunes, scrub moorland, cranberry bogs and small forests. For a guide to the trails of the area, *The Cape Cod Bike Book* is available from the two CCNS Visitors Centers. For bike rentals see *Getting Around, page 74*.

Walking

Most towns have conservation areas with marked trails (see the Tours for specifics, or contact the local Chambers of Commerce for details). There are 11 self-guided nature trails within the National Seashore of varying length and difficulty. A pamphlet describing these is available from the CCNS Visitors Centers. The many beaches also offer long pleasurable walks.

For more information on guided walks see *Nature Tours, page 76*.

Boating, sailing and windsurfing

Many places rent power boats, sailboats, windsurfers and canoes. Here are a few: **Arey's Pond Boat Yard**, S. Orleans, tel: 255-0994, offers sailing lessons; **Goose Hummock**, Orleans, tel: 255-0455, rents canoes, kayaks and Sunfishes; **Cape Cod Boats**, W. Dennis, tel: 394-9268, **Flyers Boat Rental**, Provincetown, tel: 487-0898, and **Jack's Boat Rental**, Wellfleet and Brewster, tel: 349-7553, rent a variety of crafts; **Cape Water Sports**, Harwichport, tel: 432-7079 has rentals and offers instruction.

Life's a breeze

Swimming, surfing and scuba diving

Beaches on the bay or Nantucket Sound tend to be warmer and calmer than those on the Atlantic. The Atlantic, however, sometimes offers surfing, especially after an offshore storm. All beaches listed in this book have parking avail-

able for non-residents. Check with local town halls for restrictions at town beaches.

Pump House Surf Co, Orleans, tel: 240-2226, and **Nauset Sports**, Orleans, tel: 255-4742, have boards and wet suits for sale and rent. For information on scuba diving, contact the **Aquarius Diving Center**, Buzzards Bay, tel: 759-3483, and **Cape Cod Divers**, Harwichport, tel: 432-9035.

Beach pursuits: fishing and sunbathing

Fishing, shellfishing and charter boats
Fishing is a favorite pastime on the Cape, and includes surf casting, deep-sea fishing and simply fishing the well-stocked ponds. The Chamber of Commerce publishes a *Sportsman's Guide*, detailing regulations and maps. The 'Fishing Around' column in the Friday edition of the *Cape Cod Times* will tell you what is being caught where. Shellfishing requires a permit; inquire at town halls. Charter boats leave from Falmouth Harbor, Ocean Street Docks in Hyannis, Wynchmere Harbor in Harwichport, Rock Harbor in Orleans, Town Pier in Wellfleet and MacMillan Wharf in Provincetown.

Highland Links

Golf
The temperate climate makes it possible to play golf most of the year. A 'Golf Map of Cape Cod' locating public courses is available from the Chambers of Commerce.

Horseback riding
If you want to ride horseback along a beach try the Province Lands Horse Trails in Provincetown. Stables include: **Nelson's Riding Stable**, Provincetown, tel: 487-1112; **Deer Meadow Riding Stables**, E. Harwich, tel: 432-6580; **Haland Stables**, W. Falmouth, tel: 540-2552; **Woodsong Farm**, Brewster, tel: 896-5555; **Holly Hill Farm**, Marstons Mills, tel: 428-2621.

Getting There

Opposite: Inn in Falmouth

By train

There is a weekend seasonal service on **Amtrak** (tel: (800) 872-7245) from Penn station in New York City to Buzzards Bay, Sandwich, West Barnstable and Hyannis. The train leaves early evening Friday from New York and returns Sunday night. The service runs from the end of June to the end of September.

By bus

The **Plymouth and Brockton Bus Co** (tel: 746-0378 in Plymouth, 775-5524 in Hyannis) offers a year-round service from Boston to Plymouth, Hyannis, and the Lower Cape. **Bonanza Bus Lines** (tel: 800 556-381;) has a year-round service which runs from New York City and Boston to towns on the Cape.

By ferry

There is a ferry service for foot passengers in summer only from Commonwealth Pier in Boston to Provincetown. The **Bay State Cruise Company** (tel: 617-723 7800), leaves Boston in the morning and returns in the afternoon, with a weekend service from the end of May to mid-October (tel: 487-9284) and a daily service from the end of June to the beginning of September. **Cape Cod Cruises** (tel: 747-2400) runs a service between Plymouth and Provincetown from the end of May through September.

73

A great way to arrive

By plane

Airline service can be unpredictable due to sudden changes in the weather and the small aircraft used. Barnstable County Municipal Airport in Hyannis (tel: 775-2020) have up to date information.

Cape Air (tel: 228-7695/800 352-0714) flies from Boston's Logan Airport to Barnstable Airport and Provincetown Municipal Airport year round; **Business Express/Delta Connection** (tel: 800 345-3400) flies year round from Boston and New York's La Guardia Airport to Barnstable Airport; **USAir Express** (tel: 800 428-4322) flies from Boston to Barnstable; **Colgan Air** (tel: 800 272-5488) flies from New York's La Guardia and New Jersey's Newark to Barnstable; **Continental** (tel: 800 525-0280) flies from Newark to Barnstable.

By car

The Cape Cod Canal is 60 miles (96km) from Boston on Rt 3 South and 220 miles (354km) from New York City, taking I-95, changing to I-195 at Providence, RI. Traffic is a problem on summer weekends. Avoid traveling in the late afternoon on Fridays, Sundays and holidays.

Hopper's gas station, Truro

Getting Around

By bus

Besides the Plymouth, Brockton, and Bonanza bus lines (*see Getting There, previous page*), the **Cape Cod Regional Transit Authority** offers limited services between Woods Hole ferry terminal, the Hyannis bus terminal and Barnstable Village.

All aboard for Nantucket

By ferry

Ferry services to Nantucket and Martha's Vineyard leave from Woods Hole, Hyannis and Falmouth. The **Steamship Authority** (tel: 477-8600) takes car and foot passengers year-round from Woods Hole to Oak Bluffs and Vineyard Haven on Martha's Vineyard, and from Hyannis to Nantucket. **Hy-Line Cruises** leaves from Hyannis and goes to Nantucket year-round and to Martha's Vineyard from early May to late October. **Island Queen** (tel: 548-4800) runs from Falmouth Harbor to Oak Bluffs from the end of May to mid-October.

The first US Rotary, Dennis

By car

There are three main routes along the length of the Cape. Rt 6 goes from Sandwich to Provincetown and Rt 6A, also called the Old King's Highway, parallels it as far as Orleans. This is an historic preservation district and so makes a very scenic route. Rt 28 starts in Bourne, and makes a U shape, heading south to follow Nantucket Sound before turning north to Orleans. Rt 28A is a prettier road parallelling Rt 28 from Bourne to Falmouth.

Massachusetts has many rotaries and for those not used to them they can be confusing. Cars already traveling on the rotary have the right of way, but not all local drivers abide by this, so approach with care. Massachusetts permits a right turn on a red light except where marked.

For parking within towns, look for municipal lots. For parking at town beaches, check with the town hall for eligibility requirements. For CCNS beaches, arrive early in summer as lots fill up quickly.

Car rental companies on the Cape: **Avis**, Hyannis Airport, tel: 775-2888/(800) 331-1212; **Budget**, Barnstable, tel: 771-2744; **Hertz**, Hyannis Airport, tel: 775-5825/(800) 654-3131; **Thrifty**, tel: (800) 367-2277, in Hyannis, tel: 771-0450, in Provincetown, tel: 487-9418.

By bicycle

An abbreviated list of bike rental shops: **Corner Cycle**, Falmouth, tel: 540-4195; **Cascade Motor Lodge**, Hyannis, tel: 775-9717; **Rail Trail Bike Rentals**, Brewster, tel: 896-8200; **Little Capistrano**, Eastham, tel: 255-6515; **Arnold's**, Provincetown, tel: 487-0844.

Pedal power

Facts for the Visitor

Chambers of Commerce

Cape Cod Canal Region, 70 Main Street, Buzzards Bay, tel: 759-6000; **Sandwich** has a seasonal booth on Rt 130 near Rt 6; **Falmouth**, 20 Academy Lane, tel: 548-8500, (800) 526-8532; **Mashpee**, Cape Cod 5, Box 1245, tel: 477-0792/(800) 526-8532; **Hyannis**, 1481 Rt 132, tel: 775-2201/(800) 449-6647; **Yarmouth**, 657 Rt 28, S. Yarmouth, tel: 778-1008/ (800) 732-1008; **Dennis**, corner of Rts 134 and 28, S. Dennis, tel: 398-3568/(800) 243-9920; **Brewster**, Town Hall Rt 6A ½ mile east of Rt 124; **Harwich**, Rt 28, Harwichport, tel: 432-1600; **Chatham**, 533 Main Street, tel: 945-5199; **Orleans**, Box 153, Orleans, tel: 240-2484; **Eastham**, Rt 6 near Fort Hill Area, tel: 255-3444; **Wellfleet**, Rt 6, tel: 349-2510; **Truro**, Rt 6, N. Truro, tel: 487-1288; **Provincetown**, 307 Commercial Street, tel: 487-3424; **Plymouth**, Destination Plymouth, tel: 747-4161.

Telephones

Numbers in this book are in the 508 area code unless stated.

Beach phone

Emergencies

Ambulance / Fire / Police: 911

Health

Lyme Disease: transmitted by deer ticks, this bacterial infection can be serious if left untreated, and is especially dangerous for pregnant women. The ticks live in tall grass, primarily from April to October. For prevention, wear light colored pants (the ticks are then easier to spot) tucked into socks, and long-sleeved shirts, and avoid high grass. Use DEET based insect spray for clothing and inspect for ticks. If a tick has imbedded itself in the skin, remove without squeezing its body and disinfect with alcohol. If a red-rimmed rash appears, seek medical advice.

High grass can harbor ticks

Disabled

Cape Organization for Rights of the Disabled, tel: 775-8300 supplies information on accessibility. **Cape Cod National Seashore**, tel: 349-3785 has facilities for disabled visitors. The pamphlet 'Guide to Accessible Fun in the Sun' is available from local Chambers of Commerce.

Whale watching

Provincetown is the closest harbor to Stellwagon Bank, the whales' feeding grounds, and three companies operate from here (MacMillan Wharf): **Dolphin Fleet**, tel: 349-1900/(800) 826-9300; **Portuguese Princess**, tel: 487-2651/(800) 442-3188; **Ranger V**, tel: 487-3322/(800) 992-

Dolphin-watching

Sailing charter

9333. **Hyannis Whale Watch Cruises**, tel:362-6088/ (800) 287-0374, leave from Barnstable Harbor.

Nature tours

The **Cape Cod National Seashore**, tel:255-3421, has guided walks, canoe trips and more. **Cape Cod Museum of Natural History**, tel: 896-3867, (800) 479-3867, offers tours of Monomoy Wildlife Refuge and trips to Nauset Marsh. The **Massachusetts Audubon Society**, tel: 349-2615 in Wellfleet, conducts tours to Nauset Marsh, Monomoy Island and the Ashumet Wildlife Sanctuary.

Sailing charters

Volta, a 40-ft (12.2-meter) yawl, sails out of Quissett Harbor in Falmouth and accommodates six to eight people, four for overnight (tel: 647-1554). The replica 1750s schooner, *Liberte,* offers 2-hour excursions four times a day from Falmouth Harbor (tel: 548-2626). The catboat *Eventide* offers 1½-hour excursions from Ocean Street Dock in Hyannis six times daily (tel: 775-0222). *Sabbatical,* a 31-ft (9.4-meter) ketch, sails from Saquatucket Harbor in Harwich with 3-hour, 6-hour or overnight trips (tel: 432-3416).

Dune tours

Art's Dune Tours, tel: 487-1950, runs hour-long narrated excursions by 4X4 through the National Seashore, passing dune shacks used by famous artists and writers.

Sandwich station

Railroads

The Cape Cod Scenic Railroad, tel: 771-3788, runs a vintage train service from Hyannis to Sandwich, the Cape Cod Canal and back to Hyannis. Special excursions include a romantic dinner train and ecology tours.

Cape Cod for Children

On those rainy days when you can't get to the beach, Cape Cod still has many diversions to interest children. Look for the free booklet called *Kids on the Cape* available from local Chambers of Commerce. Each town operates a recreation program (open to visitors) which includes sports, crafts and trips, and local libraries often have story hours. There are also many camps in the area for families staying a week or more (for more information write to the **Cape Cod Association of Children's Camps**, Box 38, Brewster 02631).

Here is a selective list of local attractions.

Cape Cod Children's Museum, 137 Teaticket Way, E. Falmouth, tel: 457-4667. Offers a story hour, science programs and a special bubble room for toddlers.
Cape Cod YMCA, Box Y, Rt 132, W. Barnstable, tel: 362-6500. Offers kids' evenings, day camps, swimming classes and 'fun clubs' for sports, crafts and nature.

Potato Chip Factory snacks

Cape Cod Potato Chip Factory, Independence Park, Rt 132, Hyannis, tel: 775-7253. Has free factory tours.
Zooquariun of Cape Cod, Rt 28, W. Yarmouth, tel: 775-8883. Part zoo with a petting area, and part aquarium.
Discovery Days Children's Museum, 444 Rt 28, Box 531, Dennisport, tel: 398-1600. Creative environment with hands-on exhibits, nature and science areas, story and craft hours, music room and more.
Cape Cod Museum of Natural History, 869 Rt 6A, Brewster, tel: 896-3867, (800) 479-3867 (see *Tour 5, page 35*), and the **Wellfleet Bay Wildlife Sanctuary**, Box 236, S. Wellfleet 02663, tel: 349-2615. Both offer nature-oriented activities and day camps.

Ramble in the rain

Bassett Wild Animal Farm, 620 Tubman Rd off Rt 124, Brewster, tel: 896-3224 (*see Tour 5, page 37*).
Trampoline Center, 296 Rt 28, Harwich, tel: 432-8717. Has a dozen trampolines for children to play on.
Play-a-Round Playground, Depot Road behind the Elementary School, Chatham. Designed with the input of local children, this wonderful wood structure includes a fenced in area for toddlers and an area for the disabled.
Artscape, Coles Neck Road, Wellfleet, tel: 349-6787, **Summer Center Children's Activities**, RR2 old Rt 6, Wellfleet, tel: 349-7988, and the **Truro Center for the Arts**, 10 Meetinghouse Road, Box 756, Truro, tel: 349-7511. All offer arts and crafts programs.
Harwich Junior Theatre, Box 168, W. Harwich 02671, tel: 432-2002, and **Academy of Performing Arts**, 120 Main Street, Orleans, tel: 255-5510; box office 255-1963. Theater classes; the Academy also offers music and dance classes.

Where to Stay

Accommodations on Cape Cod range from campsites, youth hostels and motor inns to guest houses, cottages, B&Bs and large resorts. It is advisable to reserve for the summer season as soon as possible, since popular establishments fill up early. Reservations services include: **House Guests Cape Cod and the Islands**, Box 1881, Orleans 02653, tel: 896-7053 or (800) 666-4678; **Bed and Breakfast Cape Cod**, Box 341, W. Hyannisport 02672, tel: 775-2772; **Provincetown Reservations System**, 293 Commercial Street, Provincetown 02657, tel: 487-4620/(800) 648-0364; **Destinations**, tel: (800) 333-4667. For house rentals contact local real estate agencies and remember that most properties are rented a year in advance.

There are three AYH hostels on the Cape: **Hyland AYH Hostel**, 465 Falmouth Rd, Hyannis; **Mid-Cape AYH Hostel**, 75 Goody Hallet Drive, Eastham, tel: 255-2785; **Hosteling International Truro**, N. Pamet Road, Truro, tel: 349-3889. There are a number of private campgrounds throughout the Cape, plus campsites in Nickerson State Park, Brewster. No camping is allowed within the National Seashore.

$ = less than $100, $$ = $100–200, $$$ = over $200 for double room per night in high season.

Truro Youth Hostel in the Old Coast Guard Station

78

Lighting the way

Sandwich and Falmouth

$$ Coonamessett Inn, 311 Gifford Street, Falmouth 02540, tel: 548-2300. An inviting traditional inn with 25 rooms and suites and landscaped grounds.

$ Dillingham House, 71 Main Street, Sandwich, tel: 833-0065, a c1650 ¾-Cape house with five guest rooms.

Barnstable Area

$ Crocker Tavern B&B, 3095 Rt 6A, Barnstable, tel: 362-5115. Three guest rooms in a restored 1750 tavern.

$-$$ Trade Winds Inn, Craigville Beach, Box 107, Craigville 02636, tel: 775-0365. Large modern motel overlooking the beach, some rooms with balconies.

$ Inn on Sea Street, 358 Sea Street, Hyannis, tel: 775-8030. One of the nicest places to stay in Hyannis, this B&B offers nine rooms in two houses. Great breakfasts.

Yarmouth and Dennis

$$ The Cove at Yarmouth, 183 Rt 28, W. Yarmouth, tel: 771-3666, reservations: (800) 228-2968. Full scale resort with all the amenities.

$-$$ Beach House Inn B&B, 61 Uncle Stephen's Road, Box 494, W. Dennis, tel: 398-4575. Right on the beach, this inn has seven rooms and access to a kitchen.

$ Isaiah Hall B&B, 152 Whig Street, Dennis, tel: 385-

Cape hideaway

9928, (800) 736-0160. A rambling 1850s farmhouse with 11 rooms and plenty of indoor and outdoor space.

Brewster, Harwich and Chatham

$ Old Manse Inn, 1861 Main Street, tel: 896-3149. There are nine guest rooms in this 1800 sea captain's house.

$ Seadar Inn By-the-Sea, Braddock Lane, Harwichport, tel: 432-0264, 430-0921, off season: 842-4525. Comfortable establishment near the beach with 23 rooms.

$$$ Chatham Bars Inn, Shore Road, Chatham, tel: 945-0096/(800) 527-4884. The quintessential old seaside resort housed in a 1914 hunting lodge, with 152 rooms, renowned restaurant and lots of extras.

Orleans and Eastham

$ Nauset House Inn, Beach Road, Box 774, E. Orleans 02643, tel: 255-2195. An 1810 farmhouse with 14 rooms and within walking distance of Nauset Beach. Best choice in the area.

$-$$ Whalewalk Inn, 220 Bridge Road, Eastham, tel: 255-0617. Eleven rooms in 1830s whaling captain's home.

Wellfleet and Truro

$ Inn at Duck Creeke, East Main Street, Box 364, Wellfleet 02667, tel: 349-9333. Inn dating from the 1800s overlooking a duck pond and a salt creek.

$ Kalmar Village, Rt 6A, Box 745, N. Truro 02652, tel: 487-0585/(617) 247-0211 in winter. Well-kept roomy cottages plus several motel rooms on private beach.

Provincetown

$ The Cape Codder, 570 Commercial Street, tel: 487-0131. Small 19th-century guesthouse with private beach.

$ Outermost Hostel, 30A Winslow Street, tel: 487-4378. Not affiliated with AYH, this hostel provides 30 bunks in five cabins at very good rates.

An option in Provincetown

Index